PRAISE FOR
CRACKING CORPORATE

"A very practical and beneficial read providing good perspective to any young professional entering the multi-dimensional corporate environment."
Noor Mahomed Sacoor
Group Strategy Director, RCL Foods

"Interesting and enjoyable read: conversational, clear and concise. The interviews, research and authors' experiences provide empowering tips and strategies for both students and graduates with a focus on career acceleration."
Tracy Smail
Leadership & Learning VP, Absa Bank

"An insightful guide filled with valuable wisdom; reading through this felt like having a chat with a very knowledgeable friend."
Vidushi, Nicole, Florence
Graduate Interns

Published by
LID Publishing
An imprint of LID Business Media Ltd.
LABS House, 15-19 Bloomsbury Way,
London, WC1A 2TH, UK

info@lidpublishing.com
www.lidpublishing.com

A member of:

BPR ⊛

businesspublishersroundtable.com

Printed by Severn, Gloucester
ISBN: 978-1-911687-62-7
ISBN: 978-1-911687-63-4 (ebook)

Cover and page design: Caroline Li

MATTHEW BUTLER-ADAM
AND YUSUF AMEER

CRACKING CORPORATE

BUILDING A CAREER THAT YOU CAN BE PROUD OF

MADRID | MEXICO CITY | LONDON
BUENOS AIRES | BOGOTA | SHANGHAI

For John, Trish and Helen,
thank you for showing me what family means.

For my parents, thank you for teaching me
the importance of helping others.
And for Nadeera, your love and encouragement
means the world to me.

CONTENTS

INTRODUCTION

If you are considering reading this book to find all the answers to your corporate dreams, just put it down now and walk away. In fact, let us tell you a few more reasons you should *not* read this book. Do not read this book if you are looking for a significant intellectual contribution in the field of business or finance. Do not read this book if you're the child of an industry heavyweight in the corporate world – you really won't learn very much more than mum and dad whispered into your ear as they tucked you in at bedtime. And most certainly do not read this book if you have any moral qualms with free market economies, or more specifically the desire to generate and accumulate wealth through significant salaried and entrepreneurial income.

Having cut our potential readership down very early on, let us spend some time explaining what this book *will* be useful for, and who might benefit most from reading it. Our intended audience is the very large cohort of first-generation employees in the corporate world. We focus on the full journey, from educational decisions to the first few years of work in a corporate role. This means you might be at the end of high school, at university, or just starting out in your first corporate internship or full-time role. To be clear, this does not mean you have to come from a low-income or seriously disadvantaged background (though you may do). It means that your parents might have been, for example, teachers or police officers (employed by the state) or domestic workers/homemakers. But you, for whatever reason, want to be a commercially-oriented professional (in a large corporate organization) – a lawyer, a banker, a management consultant or a software developer (and yes there are many more than this list). There are two reasons we think you need this book.

Firstly, without a family with private sector experience, moving into the corporate environment anywhere in the world is tough. It's kind of like learning a new language – a language that extends to how you look, how you walk, and how you make almost every decision in and about your life. Typically, you will be part of a cohort or generation whose parents never really 'get' what it is you actually do. In some ways that can be quite a funny experience (especially if they try to explain how proud they are of you to their friends and suggest that you 'run the banks') – but it can also make you feel quite lonely at home and at family events, and that's something you will need to manage.

Secondly, and this is a little more specific to emerging markets, large corporates tend to be quite far behind in developing helpful mentorship and apprenticeship cultures (with some exceptions). When implemented, these processes usually bridge the gap we talk about in point one – but, sadly, many organizations continue to embrace a 'sink or swim' culture irrespective of someone's starting point. This is where the book you're about to read becomes a game-changer. Our hope is to make your transition into the corporate world a little easier AND help you navigate your way with confidence. Additionally we think it offers some pretty damn good advice about getting to the top.

Now, let's spend a minute describing where this book fits in with what is already out there. Is this a self-help book? Though we are loath to admit it, it probably is. But rather than some generic motivational mumbo-jumbo, this book has a very specific focus on how to make it in corporate environments. On the spectrum from deeply pessimistic about making it in the corporate world to hopelessly optimistic about the upside prospects, we'd like to think this book will reflect a fair middle ground – yes, you can make it, but you'll have to accept some sacrifices. You can't have it all, but you can get pretty close. We acknowledge that this may appear as exciting as wet cardboard, especially in the context of a world of provocative titles screaming "Zero F*#ks Given!" or "Crush It 24/7!" But here's the real deal: we're not here to blast you with pump-you-up-rhetoric. We'd rather write what we genuinely believe and give you solid advice, based on experience, that will help you get ahead. And that's gold in a world that's chock-full of volatility, uncertainty, complexity, ambiguity (VUCA).

We should probably also quickly define what we mean by 'corporate' because, as you will discover, there are slightly different interpretations of what it means. Our definition is broad – very much like that of the *Cambridge Dictionary*: "relating to business, especially a large business."[1] We mean big private sector businesses – this includes tech companies, consulting houses, law firms and large business in most sectors of the economy.

Finally, you'll note that we keep saying "we" in this introduction. That's because there are two authors. We co-wrote the introduction but decided to write most of the chapters individually. This way, each of us could dive deep into the topics we're particularly well-versed in or genuinely passionate about. At the start of each chapter, you will see who the main author is (or if it's a joint effort).different experiences, so it means we can offer more than a single perspective throughout. Ultimately, we felt that the split authorship would be beneficial to you, the reader, as it has meant that you get to hear from two different people with different experiences. This also means we can offer more than a single perspective throughout the book. By blending our distinct insights, our aim is to provide you with a multi-dimensional perspective that not only deepens your understanding but also empowers you to thrive in the corporate realm.

A NOTE ON (OUR) PRIVILEGE

MATT

Now you might be reading this thinking, how on earth can a guy with the name Matthew Butler-Adam (not to mention the middle name William) have anything to say to you as the reader (a first-generation entrant into the corporate world)? To that, I say, fair point, and it's certainly worth talking about. I'm going to say three things about this.

Firstly, I'm very aware of the privileged position I hold as a middle-class White man (my parents were in education, not corporate, but I had all the benefits of a happy upbringing). If anything, I've been made increasingly aware of it by being in a corporate setting. This puts me in a unique position – I see many of the advantages I have, so I can speak to them directly. I've had the 'friend' from college give me a tip before an interview or the peer at work who made sure I came prepared to a certain meeting (that other people may have thought was routine). There are probably parts of my privilege I don't even know about, but the stuff

I am aware of is the stuff I want to talk about in this book. I want to share with you all the things I do (or don't do) that I'm not sure everyone else is aware of when they start working. At the same time I definitely didn't have the advice and network I could see some of my peers had and that mostly arose because their parents (or other close family members) were well-established in the corporate world. I would definitely describe myself as first-generation corporate. I hope that makes sense – it was tough to write.

Secondly, Yusuf and I have both mentored, coached and worked with many first-generation corporate professionals. While we like to think we've helped them along in some small way, for the most part, they have reminded us how hard those first few years can be. We use these conversations as a way of bridging the gap – many of the things we talk about in this book came from those discussions, along with our own experiences. We think these discussions helped those young professionals, and we think they will help our readers too.

Thirdly, and now I'm speaking for both of us, we checked ourselves. We turned to peers who were also first generation, who were not White, who were women and who were all three, and asked for their advice. They pushed our thinking – we learned a great deal (and there is still more for us to learn, by the way). We updated the way we framed and discussed key points. To them, we owe a great debt. Thank you! On top of this, especially affecting *Chapter 1*, we interviewed working professionals who weren't like us – who had other perspectives and different backgrounds. We share *their* key thoughts on the topic of 'purpose' early

in the book, and these thoughts guide most of the narrative throughout.

YUSUF

I am a fourth-generation South African-born man of Indian descent. While I did not experience the same privilege as a White man, I have nonetheless been fortunate enough to be privileged in other ways. I'm conscious that this gives me an advantage over many people coming into the corporate world today.

I was lucky enough to have parents who were both professionals (but they did not work in corporate). We lived in a modest house in a suburb that was designated for 'Indians' during apartheid South Africa, and I, like Matt, had the comforts of a middle-class upbringing. But, growing up as a brown person in the 1990s in South Africa, it was also clear to me what I did not have. I didn't have access to influential people within my social network, people who held commanding positions in the corporate world, or people who could offer advice and guidance and make the all-important introductions for me. I didn't have friends who could casually take a gap year after school to backpack through Europe before chasing their passions, detached from the need to hastily launch a career in order to secure financial stability. And that confidence and self-assuredness that seems to ooze effortlessly from the truly privileged? I certainly didn't have that either!

At the time, I bemoaned all the things that I did not have – yes, I was that guy. But now, looking back, I realize that the genesis of this book was in the things I did *not* have. I learned to leverage the things that I did have so that I could position myself to get the things that I didn't. This did not happen overnight. It took many years of contending with setbacks and failures, dealing with insecurities and impostor syndrome, to discover my own sense of worth and my place in the world. At this point along the journey, I felt it necessary to share my learnings and experiences in a lasting and meaningful way so that you, the reader, can enhance your own skills and abilities to reach your desired outcomes, regardless of where you are on the privilege spectrum.

CHAPTER 1

ON PURPOSE: START WITH THE END IN MIND

BY MATT AND YUSUF

WHY START WITH PURPOSE?

We start this book by talking about purpose in the broadest terms. The reason is very simple – every bit of advice we give in the subsequent chapters will be influenced by the purpose you envision for yourself. Your purpose is fundamentally your reason for being, so it includes the present, and it also should include some of the objectives and goals you see for yourself in the future.

We worked as strategy consultants for many years and so we feel compelled to start with a strategy framework – we believe that your personal purpose is a choice and is therefore a strategic matter. Before you start making decisions about what you study and where you work, you should have *some* sense of the destination you are working towards. This isn't at all easy, of course, and some people don't know what they really want to do for the greater part (if not all) of their life.

The good news is you don't have to have the final answer figured out early on. What you do need to do is to start thinking about this topic – with a view to keep learning and refine your answer as you journey through life and gain more experience. Remember, it's never too early to start thinking about your purpose and where you'd like to see yourself professionally a few years from now.

Some of you may already have the end in sight and that's great – to this group, all we'd say is keep an open mind. Life has a way of changing the way you see things, and a mid-career switch might be on the cards. Some of you may feel purposeless and that's also perfectly okay – but you absolutely need to start thinking about this topic. We reckon the best way to help you navigate your purpose comes from talking to professionals with successful and purpose-driven careers. As part of our preparation for writing this book, we spent time with six business leaders who shared their ideas about purpose and how it influenced their career journey. We summarize some of the key insights here.

TALKING TO PROFESSIONALS ABOUT THEIR PURPOSE

We interviewed six professionals with powerful career stories: Ruwayda Redfearn, CEO of Deloitte Africa; Imtiaz Patel, chairman of MultiChoice Group; Monde Nkosi, Stanford graduate and director at the hedge fund Value Capital Partners; Sharmla Chetty, banking professional and CEO of Duke Corporate Education, USA; Vivek Ramsaroop, partner at a large global law firm and currently based in London; and Mohammad Chowdhury, partner in the consulting industry with a focus on digital transitions, and currently based in Australia.

We spent some time chatting to these professionals about how they went about navigating their careers. We hope their stories inspire and encourage you.

RUWAYDA REDFEARN
– CEO OF DELOITTE AFRICA

Raised in Chatsworth, Durban, by factory worker parents who emphasized education, Ruwayda Redfearn's journey from a humble background to becoming the CEO of Deloitte Africa is a testament to ambition, resilience and the power of education. Her early exposure to business operations at a clothing factory ignited her passion for entrepreneurship, steering her away from a potential medical career towards becoming a chartered accountant. Constantly embracing her connection to her roots, she used her early understanding of business operations in her ascent, evolving her personal purpose through various life experiences, from motherhood to surviving a medical crisis.

Today, as the CEO of Deloitte Africa, Ruwayda navigates the demands of the present and those of the future under her strategy, "Purpose Beyond Profit." Aiming to solve African challenges from within, she firmly believes that the continent's destiny lies in the hands of African leaders. Ruwayda remains an advocate for the potential of Africa, continually strategizing to realize her vision for the continent. She underscores the significance of seeking opportunities to make a difference, encouraging the next generation to prioritize usefulness to their family, society and the continent over personal success.

We asked Ruwayda about her personal purpose and how it has evolved over time. Here is what she had to say:

> I had no clue why I wanted to become a chartered accountant and what my purpose was at 17 or 18 years old. The current generation of 17- and 18-year-olds think a lot more broadly around purpose and what the roles of corporate communities are, and what their roles are individually. They think about a lot more than I did all those years ago. I think purpose evolves over time.

We also asked how her purpose had changed:

> When I became a mother, four and a half years ago, my perspective changed. Even prior to that, when I went through a medical crisis and was faced with a life-threatening disease, my perspective changed. Experience and age change how and why we do things.
>
> I believe that humanity is at a tipping point – the leadership that is emerging is very different from what humanity has experienced over the past centuries. This next round of leaders has a critical role to play in redefining leadership globally. They do not have to look to the past to define good leadership; they need to define it for themselves.

In our view, Ruwayda shows us that your purpose can change but that it is becoming an increasingly important concept for leaders to consider.

IMTIAZ PATEL
– CHAIRMAN OF MULTICHOICE GROUP

Imtiaz Patel's journey – from the racially charged town of Schweizer-Reneke, South Africa, during the apartheid era to becoming the non-executive chairman of MultiChoice Group – is a narrative of resilience, adaptability and a deep commitment to social change. He was moulded by the paradoxical experience of operating a family business catering to a White clientele while enduring marginalization in his own town. Imtiaz's early trials – including witnessing the destruction of his family business in 1982, sharing a bed with a relative due to financial constraints and eventually reorienting his career from dentistry to teaching in Soweto – fostered his determination and dreams of a different future.

Despite an initial setback in his aspiration to become the CEO of the cricket team Gauteng, Imtiaz channelled his disappointment into propelling his career forward. He honed his commercial acumen as the Director of Professional Cricket for Gauteng and earned a pivotal role at SuperSport, setting the stage for his ascension to group CEO of the MultiChoice Group. Now, as the non-executive chairman of MultiChoice, Imtiaz's role includes steering the company in an industry disrupted by streaming giants such as Amazon and Netflix. Throughout his career, Imtiaz has held fast to his foundational purpose – uplifting the underprivileged and transforming his community. This dedication is demonstrated in his instrumental role in reshaping MultiChoice. The company, once overwhelmingly White at 99%, has undergone a transformative shift, now boasting an 87% Black workforce.

Imtiaz spoke to the importance of purpose to him and how it evolves over time:

Purpose is very important to me and guides all that I do. Firstly, on a foundational level, my purpose revolves around my family, my community and society at large. Fundamentally, I am African, and I'm very conscious of that. This means that as someone in a position of power, I have a responsibility to give back and help to uplift those that are coming from unprivileged backgrounds. But it's not about handouts – it's more about mentoring and providing opportunities to those that are deserving. Secondly, I think about how I can create lasting systems that serve to uplift people over the long term. How do I plant the seeds of trees that I may never see the fruits of? And thirdly, a core part of my purpose is my family. If my family is not in good shape, well everything really starts to fall apart. So, I spend a lot of time to ensure that my family and their well-being are prioritized. The point here is that my foundational purpose is something that is bigger than me – it's something that is impactful to my country, my society and the people around me.

Now, as we go through life, we will enter different phases as the hierarchy of our needs will evolve. For example, when you start a new career, you just want to look after yourself. That will likely then evolve to providing for your family, then progress to building wealth, perhaps, and to securing your and your family's future. This is what I call the dynamic purpose. Professionally speaking for me right now, my dynamic purpose is directed towards developing current management and future leaders of MultiChoice. I need to ensure that I help them to thrive over the long term so they can also hand over batons of success to future generations of leaders while creating a continuity of success in the business to make an impact on Africa as a whole.

For Imtiaz, purpose is a central theme in his life. It forms a part of his identity and encapsulates his responsibilities towards his family, community, and professional role at MultiChoice, reflecting a philosophy that extends beyond himself.

MONDE NKOSI
– DIRECTOR AT VALUE CAPITAL PARTNERS

Monde was raised in South Africa in the KwaZulu-Natal province. He was born in Jozini, northern KwaZulu-Natal, and then lived in Pietermaritzburg and Durban. He was part of a big family. Monde's father was an entrepreneur.

Monde was raised in a home where education was very important. His mother and grandmother were both teachers and his mother started a school. Monde believes he had some great breaks in life (while that may be true, we think that he also worked really hard!). He went to a good high school on a scholarship and was the head prefect. He studied at the University of Cape Town and completed a Bachelor of Business Science majoring in finance. He then went to Stanford and studied for a Master of Arts in Education and an MBA.

Today Monde is an executive director at Value Capital Partners, the leading activist investment firm in South Africa. He is also a non-executive director of several listed companies, including ADvTECH, which is Africa's largest listed education company, and Lesaka Technologies, which is a financial technology business.

We asked Monde about his purpose. He had this to say:

> I have two fundamental beliefs that drive my purpose. Firstly, I'm a deep believer in the power of capitalism to drive human progress. That's why I spend my days working on how to make companies better.
>
> Let's take a simple example: MTN has brought cellphone access to 272 million people in countries

such as South Africa, Nigeria, Ghana, Uganda and South Sudan, in both rural and urban areas. That has made a huge impact in people's lives, in their ability to stay connected with loved ones, in their ability to participate in a modern economy. Now imagine if, instead of a private for-profit company like MTN, it had been the government providing the service. How many people do we believe would have cellphone coverage? How efficient would the service be? So when I work on making businesses better, I look to the end goal of what I'm doing. When a company like ADvTECH does well, that impacts its 80,000 students, who get a better and cheaper education. When Lesaka does well, more people have access to financial services that many of us take for granted.

Secondly, [I believe] in the power of education. Education has played a huge role in my life and in my family's path over the past three generations. At an individual level and at a country level, we need greater access to high-quality education. I'm very lucky that I get to marry my passions in my job because education is one of the investment sectors that I cover.

Monde has a clear vision about the way value is created in the private sector and actively wants to support efforts to increase that value. He is also very clear about the power of education to help individuals support those markets.

SHARMLA CHETTY
– CEO OF DUKE CORPORATE EDUCATION, USA

The indignity of apartheid was made real to Sharmla Chetty at the age of five, when she first went Christmas shopping with her grandmother in Durban's main department store. They were barred from entering the restaurant:

> I was hungry, and she wanted me to have something to eat [and] I saw the tears rolling down her face.

Sharmla also recalls having to fight to get a second-hand pair of shoes to support her passion for running.

Even though she describes her upbringing as middle class, Sharmla faced a very difficult environment. She was expelled from high school for her vocal opposition to the apartheid regime. Today she is CEO of Duke Corporate Education, Duke University's executive education arm, top in the Financial Times 2023 ranking of custom executive education programmes.[2]

Sharmla has purpose at the centre of her work, as she shares here:

> I believe that my role is contributing to changing lives. I prefer to say I'm a chief purpose officer as opposed to a CEO because we're in the business of connecting people to their purpose. We're in the business of transforming lives. We're in the business of creating meaning. For me that's what matters.

I think my purpose is really around equality. This has evolved over time – starting as an activist and now as a CEO. It really is a sense of being inclusive, a sense of belonging. That's what purpose is. The second piece around purpose is around empathy and trust. For me it's also about creating the psychological safety required for an individual to actually become better. This extends to making companies better, making communities better and overall making a better society for all of us to live in.

Sharmla shows us that it's possible to combine business excellence with the desire to make society better for everyone.

VIVEK RAMSAROOP
– LAWYER PRACTISING M&A

Vivek grew up in South Africa and was raised by his mother. He went to high school in KwaZulu-Natal and attended the University of Cape Town. Today, Vivek is a lawyer in a premier M&A (mergers and acquisitions) practice. He has experience in all aspects of cross-border African transactions and a focus on downstream private equity. He finds creative and innovative ways to solve complicated legal and other issues that arise in the context of deal-making in Africa. He manages complicated project workstreams, plays a leading role in negotiations and holds the pen on key legal agreements. He also mentors and trains junior lawyers in his practice.

Vivek shares an interesting take on purpose that might resonate with you:

> Purpose is an overwhelming and exhausting concept. At university, I was obsessed with discovering my purpose, and felt a great deal of anxiety that despite studying widely and being deeply involved in a bunch of projects that I was passionate about, no clear purpose was emerging – not in the way it is described by leadership gurus and self-help books.
>
> I'm in my tenth year of practising law, and still no revelations, unfortunately. I do have a clearer sense of the components of the life I want – solid relationships, health and career. It is a constant struggle to get the right balance, and it shifts as you grow up.

So, just remember, pondering purpose may not always yield quick answers. And that's okay – Vivek's journey teaches us that it is engagement that truly matters.

MOHAMMAD CHOWDHURY
– FOUNDER AND CEO AT
LONG STREET ADVISORS

Born and raised in South London by parents who emigrated from East Pakistan (now Bangladesh), Mohammad Chowdhury's upbringing was a kaleidoscope of cultural diversity, economic challenges and exposure to systemic inequality. His parents, despite working laborious jobs, prioritized education and sent him to a private school, offering him a plethora of academic opportunities. Facing the harsh realities of racism, he felt like an outsider both at school and within his family community. This dual experience stirred his interest in politics, philosophy and economics, which he studied at the University of Oxford, aiming to comprehend and mitigate the systemic inequalities that had been integral to his early life.

Today, Mohammad stands as a global leader in digital transformation and the CEO of Long Street Advisors, a consultancy that specializes in digital transformation. He consults on executing large-scale digitization programmes and serves on the boards of organizations that resonate with his mission, such as the Institute for the Future of Work in the UK, the Australian Institute of International Affairs and a technology company in Bangladesh. His career, driven by a purpose anchored in his personal experiences, centres on fostering digital connectivity to facilitate economic growth, competitiveness and job creation, particularly in regions where such efforts can have a significant impact. His journey, from fundamental economic work to formulating strategies for digitizing entire industries and nations, is confronted with complex stakeholder dynamics and global politics.

Mohammad shares practical advice for young professionals struggling with purpose:

> If you're grappling with your purpose, then you're in a good place. If you're not, then it might mean you've wrongly assumed you know what your purpose is and how it's applied through your career – or that you're in a career that's perhaps not driven by purpose but by other goals. These possibilities might just mean your satisfaction with your career is not sustainable.
>
> So, my advice would be to choose your own adventure and the journey that fits it. Only you can do that, because you know what the adventure is that suits you, and you know how you can get to the destination you seek. There is never only one route.
>
> Don't get stuck on analysis, aiming to 'solve' what your purpose is, but rather let it come to you over time and let your appreciation of it evolve. Discuss and explore your purpose with others around you, and include a variety and diversity of perspectives that will challenge you to think harder about it. At first, do more careful listening on this, and less justifying and explaining – things to save until you're later down the track.

Mohammad's advice gives hope to those (like me) who are struggling with purpose. Don't push it, but rather keep exploring your curiosities, the things you are genuinely interested in, and have patience while you engage with new and diverse perspectives. Your purpose will naturally take shape and crystallise as you go.

KEY LEARNINGS FROM THESE INTERVIEWS

We didn't expect such different answers to our question on purpose, but they show us a few things. Firstly, you can be successful and ambitious and still be yourself – the six people defined different purposes for themselves, and you should define one for yourself too. Secondly, the maturity and complexity of your purpose can vary – we have examples above of very specific purposes but also examples where there is space for change and evolution. Finally, and most importantly, every single interviewee was actively engaged in the work required to define their purpose and involved in a discussion about it. We therefore encourage you to do the same.

Overall, we believe that having a sense of purpose is important for young professionals because it provides direction, motivation and fulfilment. When you have a clear understanding of *why* you are doing what you are doing, it helps you to stay focused on your goals and gives you a sense of meaning and satisfaction in your work.

Here are a few reasons why purpose is important:

- **Purpose provides motivation:** When you have a sense of purpose, it can motivate you to work harder and strive for success. Purpose gives you a reason to get up in the morning and tackle the challenges of the day.
- **Purpose increases job satisfaction:** When you feel that your work is meaningful and aligned with your values and interests, it can lead to greater job satisfaction. Purpose helps you feel more connected to your work and the people you work with, which can lead to a greater sense of fulfilment.
- **Purpose helps with decision-making:** When you have a clear sense of purpose, it can help to guide your decision-making. You can ask yourself whether a particular opportunity or project aligns with your purpose and use that as a guide to whether to pursue it.
- **Purpose builds resilience:** When you have a strong sense of purpose, it can help you weather the ups and downs of your career. When things get tough, you can rely on your sense of purpose to keep you going and remind you of why you started in the first place.

In a nutshell, having a sense of purpose can help you navigate your career with greater clarity, motivation and fulfilment.

CHAPTER 2

GET ORGANIZED

BY MATT

CHARLES THE GREAT

Have you ever met someone and been in complete awe? I'm sure you have, but let me tell you about a guy I met in the investment banking sector. Let's call the guy Charles. Charles had a bachelor's degree from the University of Cambridge and was already in a very senior position at a prestigious investment banking firm in his thirties. Let's just say that if he wanted to, he could buy a very nice sports car with cash and not flinch about it.

What I haven't told you is that Charles was also a semi-professional athlete. In particular, he was able to place among the professionals at international triathlon events. Without going into detail, in general the only people who are able to place so high at these events are full-time professionals – people who dedicate most of their time to the sport and use it to make a living.

To be a successful investment banker and a professional-level triathlete is almost unheard of. Surely the guy was a creep with no personal life? What I found hard to believe was that, in addition to all this, he was happily married to a woman with her own successful career (who could also have a write-up like the one above), with one kid.

What enabled Charles to live a life like this? I can't answer the question perfectly but there are at least two factors. Firstly, he came from a place of (some) privilege. He wasn't born wealthy, but he was (and still is) a White man who grew up in the developed world (probably with a stable home). So, the lottery of life had played its cards and he'd had a pretty good start (way better than most). Call this very big bucket of stuff the 'unchosen' or endowment factor in his success. But there's no way this fully explains his achievements – it is only one part of the story.

The second thing about Charles was that he was intensely structured and deliberate about his life. He left very little to chance – every element and every minute of every day was optimized. Charles didn't just have a list of goals he was going after. No, Charles – and later his wife – had an 'Excel spreadsheet life model.' The model was built to help them make decisions that would maximize their life goals – financial or otherwise. I didn't ever see the model, but it would, for example, help them think about career choices, when they would have their first child (which was a financial decision) and even where they would live. Was this too much? Were they crazy? Was it a sacrifice worth making given the lives they wanted? I don't know – but it's a pretty cool story.

I concede that this is a crazy level of structure, or even control, and many of us (myself included) would probably not be able to go to this extent. The point, however, is that Charles had massive personal and professional success, and one of the main reasons he was able to achieve this was because he imposed ridiculous structure on his life. This is not always possible, but it can easily be argued that these are the lengths you need to go to for that level of success.

BUT WHAT IF
YOU'RE NOT CHARLES?

I'm going to break structure down a bit now, so that you can understand how to develop the level of structure you need to achieve the amount of success you desire. If you were not as fortunate as Charles to be born into privilege and have a good head start, that is perfectly fine. The world is full of people who came from nothing and achieved huge success, and structure is a big part of their stories.

What's important is to understand your own unique skills and traits, as well as your quirks and idiosyncrasies. These are the things that make you, well, you. Understanding them means you can develop a structure that is aligned with your intrinsic attributes. This is by no means an easy task, but there are some clever tools that have been developed and refined over many years to help you understand this somewhat elusive concept – your personality.

FRAMEWORKS FOR CATEGORIZING PEOPLE

Most large organizations like to use any one of a host of tools to categorize their employees based on their personality types. There are two tools that I particularly like (though there are many more): the Enneagram and the Myers-Briggs Type Indicator (MBTI).

The Enneagram is a personality categorization system that focuses on how people conceptualize the world and deal with their emotions.[3] The Enneagram model describes nine personality types. You can do the test quite quickly and see what type you are (just look up a free test on the internet). The nine types are:

1. The Reformer: the rational, idealistic type
2. The Helper: the caring, interpersonal type
3. The Achiever: the success-oriented, pragmatic type
4. The Individualist: the sensitive, withdrawn type
5. The Investigator: the intense, cerebral type
6. The Loyalist: the committed, security-oriented type
7. The Enthusiast: the busy, fun-loving type

8. The Challenger: the powerful, dominating type
9. The Peacemaker: the easy-going, self-effacing type

I'm a Challenger, which means I ruffle feathers some-times. There are multiple critiques of the Enneagram system, and I haven't seen it used in many businesses, but I've seen it implemented as a useful tool for both self-reflection and team-building. However, users must understand that it offers a high-level guide and not a completely accurate personality assessment. In my opinion, most of us exhibit a blend of several, if not all, of these traits, but the model strives to pinpoint the dominant one. For instance, if you're classified as an Investigator, it doesn't imply you lack compassion.

The MBTI is an introspective self-report tool that reveals differing preferences in how people perceive the world and make decisions.[4] In other words, it tries to do the same thing that the Enneagram system does (although it pre-dates the Enneagram). The original versions of the MBTI were constructed by two Americans, Katharine Cook Briggs and her daughter Isabel Briggs Myers, and it is based on the conceptual framework proposed by Swiss psychiatrist Carl Jung. The modern and most popular version aims to find out whether people prefer to deal with:

- People and things (Extraversion or 'E') or ideas and information (Introversion or 'I')
- Facts and reality (Sensing or 'S') or possibilities and potential (Intuition or 'N')
- Logic and truth (Thinking or 'T') or values and relationships (Feeling or 'F')
- A lifestyle that is well-structured (Judgement or 'J') or one that goes with the flow (Perception or 'P')

There are 16 possible combinations (4 × 4), each with a detailed description. I, for example, am an INTJ. Probably the most fun to be had with the MBTI is to spend hours looking up what celebrities, Harry Potter characters or animals are 'your type.' In my case, the answers to those questions (respectively) are John Nash (happy about that), Draco Malfoy (I am not into Harry Potter but I know enough to understand that Malfoy sucks) and a tiger (feel great about this one!).

For all the cynics reading this, let me clear: although the ideas behind the MBTI resemble some psychological theories, it is often classified as pseudoscience (i.e. it's not very rigorous). The test has significant psychometric deficiencies, notably including poor validity (i.e. not measuring what it purports to measure) and poor reliability (i.e. giving different results for the same person on different occasions). It also has measuring categories that are not independent (i.e. some of the traits have been noted to correlate with each other), and it isn't comprehensive (it omits neuroticism, commonly deemed to be an important trait).[5]

Here's my view: the MBTI isn't perfectly accurate, and it is quite easy to dismantle it from a strictly academic perspective. However, in my experience, the MBTI is quite useful for generating a good discussion about working styles. In small team settings, I think this adds significant value – both for individual employees and in terms of the overall functioning of a team.

Now, after much blabbing and some academic gymnastics, guess what? I'm finally going to get to the point! Of all the dimensions and characteristics described by these tools, there is one distinction that has always been deeply important to me and it's the distinction between

'J' and 'P' in the MBTI. To describe this distinction in simple terms, if you prefer your life to be planned and well structured, then your preference is for 'Judgement' (this is not to be confused with 'judgemental,' which is quite a different concept and not included in the MBTI). If you prefer to go with the flow, to maintain flexibility and respond to things as they arise, then your preference is for 'Perception.'

Lots can be said about this distinction but what I think matters most is that having *some* structure in your life will help you immensely! Someone who is assessed as a 'J' is more than likely *predisposed* to imposing structure on their work and personal life, while this is a little less natural to someone characterized as a 'P.' Funnily enough, many 'J's are embarrassed about their structured nature – they feel it's something they need to apologize for (I certainly did). My advice is simple:

- **'J's:** Use your predisposition to be structured and don't be ashamed of it – just make sure you aren't so rigid that you can't act in an agile manner.
- **'P's:** Just get over it – convince yourself that some structure will help, end of story! If you struggle to do this, ask around for help. Pick a simple initial task and design a plan or structure to get going.

As a side note, I'd describe myself as having moderate OCD. For years I hated the fact that I was obsessive about structure. In a funny way, my dealing with this aspect of my personality in some ways followed the classic stages of dealing with grief. It started with denial – I refused to believe I was structured and acted as if I wasn't, to the extent that I would actively look for opportunities to prove how chaotic (and wild) my life was.

Yes, shame on me! Once I acknowledged that I was obsessive about structure, I started to apologize profusely for it – I was sad and ashamed about the fact that I needed to stick to a strict routine. Then I got angry: "Screw anyone for telling me what to do. Here's my crazy and rigid structure – take it or leave it." This was a very painful stage for anyone who worked with me. Finally, the golden age dawned where I own my structured nature but am flexible when I need to be. Wow – it took so many years to get it right!

DEVELOPING YOUR LIFE STRUCTURE

Instead of worrying about how I might be perceived by others – including you, the reader – I realized that some version of this type of thinking has actually worked well in getting me to where I am today and that, with further growth, it should stand me in good stead for where I still want to go. So, what has this meant at a practical level?

My life is organized into three parts, the first of which has some sub-parts:

1. My personal life
   a. My relationships with family and close friends
   b. My health (physical and mental)
   c. My financial situation (underneath this I have a catch-all label termed 'administrative,' which includes all the miscellaneous painful stuff around licences, key documents, taxes and many more – the list seems to get longer as I get older)

2. My learning and creative life (no sub-parts here but this includes a host of things: my education, both academic and career focused; anything I am reading; and anything I am writing, such as this very book)
3. My corporate life, or my career

Importantly, I think you should spend some time coming up with a structure that works for you. There are many useful ways of organizing your life and your thoughts – take this as an example and adjust it in a way that suits your circumstances and temperament. My structure, simple as it looks, evolved a lot over the ten years it took before I felt it was right for me. The priority order of your structure also matters, so pay attention to that.

Let me talk about each of these components, to give you more of a sense of what they include. The first category is my personal life, which for me includes three key areas: my relationships (with family, others, and yes, myself); my health (both physical and mental well-being); and my financial and administrative situation. My personal life is first on the list because it's the most important. Does this mean I spend most of my time on personal stuff? No! Sadly not – the world isn't organized well enough to allow us to do that (unless we are very, very lucky and born very rich!). But what it does mean is that I have a few rules:

- Personal stuff is something I *must* do every day (even if it's just for a short time)
- When I'm able to dedicate substantial time to personal matters, they get my full attention and energy
- If something in this category feels like it is heading into crisis mode, it gets prioritized immediately

I haven't set many goals for this personal category – it's more that I know it deserves a lot of attention. The only exception is category 1c, where I have some very high-level financial goals. I'm also aware that the way I think about the first category overall will change – for example, at this stage in my life, I don't have kids.

The second category includes all my learning, academic and creative activities. Here, I usually have some very explicit goals. Possibilities from my past and present include:

- Get accepted for a university degree
- Complete a university degree
- Complete a short online course
- Read three books this month
- Write a book

Because we live in a world that is quickly changing, I expect I will always have new goals and tasks coming up in this area – that's what keeps me engaged, excited and interested in the world around me.

The third category includes all activities related to my career. Possible goals here, again from both my past and my present, include:

- Apply for three internships this summer
- Get a job offer in a certain industry
- Get a first promotion in two years' time
- Complete an important project for my company
- Mentor at least one person in my team and make a big difference in their life
- Build and launch a new product

Even though this category is last on the list, it occupies most of my time (unless I include sleep in the personal category – which I probably should, now that I think about it).

The system works very well for me, and I encourage you to adopt some version of it for two reasons. Firstly, it takes the chaos of the world around me and puts it into three neat buckets. Of course, dig deep into each and you'll find uncertainty and complexity, but I can always look back to my structure for clarity. Secondly, it forces me to continuously set goals and work towards them. I can honestly say that many of the good things I've achieved are thanks to the practice of goal-setting, supported by a simple plan to achieve those goals.

If you're sold on this route, let me give you two final pieces of advice. Firstly, try to make your structure mutually exclusive and completely exhaustive (sometimes referred to as 'MECE'). This means the items that fit into each category *only* fit into one category: the categories can't overlap, and you shouldn't have debates about which category something goes into – it should be clear. Secondly, make sure your structure is simple. I like mine because it just has three main categories and it's super-easy to remember. You'll have a different way of thinking about life and its priorities for sure – but don't let the complexity of the world you live in stop you from developing a neat and simple structure. Oh and by the way, my structure didn't just arrive in my head fully formed – I had versions of it that continually changed over a ten-year period. The version above is a result of that iteration and constant pressure testing, and it has now been serving me well for about three years. But no doubt, as life continues and changes, I'll be making updates, and so should you.

A FINAL CASE
FOR STRUCTURE

Let me make one final argument for imposing some structure on your life and give you an example of how one person used a simple principle to focus their decision-making. The modern world is full of noise. There is so much going on – so many explicit and implicit demands on, and interruptions to, your lives on a daily basis – that at times it is hard to exercise control over what we spend your time doing. While there are upsides to flexibility and being open to spontaneity (so don't completely shut down the possibility), it also significantly limits your ability to achieve *your* goals.

A very senior and well-respected partner at an American management consulting firm once told me that he ignored most emails, only replying to ones from people he knew extremely well, and that he looked at his inbox only once a day (not throughout the day, as most people would do). When I asked why he did this and how he managed to continue his career, he said two things. Firstly, in principle, he believed that almost every email he got was from someone trying to take his time away from him to help them pursue their own ends. He decided he wanted to have much more control over how he spent his time, so he took a very strict approach to email (this is not to say he wasn't a team player). Secondly, and specifically in relation to how he got away with this approach, the answer was a little more simple and blunt: he was very senior and very good at his job, so he just could. That is a tough one for the rest of us to face up to – it might be a few more years before we can operate like that. Nonetheless, it is clear that there is a real upside to exercising more control over how we spend our time.

Having a structure to your life enables you to assess whether something you are doing or worrying about actually fits in with your priorities or whether it is just some side show – just like the partner above prioritized his emails. You can't do everything well, but you can shoot the lights out with a few things. And having a structure that you stick to will (almost always) drastically improve your odds of doing so.

I'd argue that it's useful to be structured and organized for a few reasons.

Firstly, being organized helps you to manage your time effectively. You can prioritize tasks, set clear goals, and create schedules or to-do lists. This enables you to work more efficiently, meet deadlines and accomplish your work in a timely manner. With a well-structured approach, you can avoid wasting time on unnecessary activities and focus on what truly matters.

Secondly, being organized contributes to a professional and competent image. Employers value employees who can manage their work effectively, meet deadlines consistently and produce high-quality results. When you demonstrate organization skills, it reflects positively on your reliability and ability to handle responsibilities, increasing your chances of career advancement and professional growth.

Finally, being organized facilitates professional development and growth. With effective organization, you can track your progress, identify areas for improvement and set goals for career advancement. This allows you to keep records of your achievements, skills you have acquired and feedback you have received, which can be valuable for performance evaluations, job applications and future opportunities.

CHAPTER 3

LEARN FOR LIFE

BY MATT AND YUSUF

THE JOB TO BE DONE
– YUSUF

Life is a cacophony of discordant noises that need to be turned into an elegant symphony. Teasing out this symphony requires us to solve a lot of problems. Some are small (preparing a meal); some are big (finding and pursuing a meaningful career); some are painful (removing a tooth); some are pleasurable (enjoying a refreshing drink on a hot day). The late great innovation guru and Harvard Business School professor Clayton M. Christensen defined these problems as "the jobs to be done."[6]

When we buy a product, we are essentially 'hiring' it to do a job for us – it creates a specific *value* for us that we are prepared to pay for. The same is true when it comes to corporates and their employees – people are compensated with money and other benefits (medical aid, holidays, promotions) because they create (or are expected to create) some specific value by solving the problems that are defined by the jobs they are hired to do. For all intents and purposes, the more value you can create, the higher the compensation you can demand.

The challenge, however, is that the definition of value in the corporate world is often complex and unclear. There is a plethora of defined and undefined problems that an employee must solve, and known and unknown tasks that they must carry out in order to succeed. Let me then warn you that while employment contracts and job descriptions provide rules and regulations, basic expectations and outcomes that you will be measured against, they are notoriously unreliable at sufficiently articulating the full extent of the expectations of the job and the role that you will play in the organization you work for.

Most people are hopelessly unaware of this. The result is that the vast majority of people who enter the corporate world will not achieve the level of success they envisage. This is not because they are lacking in intelligence or capability – on the contrary, many who fall short possess exceptional talents and academic achievements. Rather, they lack the understanding of *how to invest appropriately in themselves and consequently create the specific value that is required* to survive and thrive in the exciting, but complex, corporate world.

Fortunately, you don't have to be that person. This chapter will provide you with essential details about investing in yourself that you are not likely to learn anywhere else. It will give you the real deal on what value is and how it is perceived in the corporate world. It will provide you with a blueprint for how to cultivate and deliver that value, consistently, so that you can make a massive impact in your job, maximize the compensation you can command and hopefully achieve the level of success you desire.

A SHORT STORY: BUYING A FRIDGE

- YUSUF

Early on in my career, I moved to the beautiful city of Cape Town in South Africa to take up a position with a global shipping and logistics conglomerate. It was the first time that I had moved away from home and I was young and 'green,' so the prospect of being in a new city far away from comfort and familiarity was thrilling and terrifying at the same time.

I rented a small, semi-furnished studio apartment in the city that had most of the essential furniture items. But one thing it didn't have was a fridge. So, shortly after landing in Cape Town, I set off on a mission to find a fridge with only two clear objectives – it would have to fit into my tiny apartment, and it would have to fit into my very tight budget.

When I got to the store, I instinctively made my way to the budget end of the long row of fridges – the end where the smaller, cheaper and usually white fridges stand. I glanced up the row and noticed that the fridges in the line were shinier and more impressive the further along the row they were. At the end of the row, there was this stately looking double-door behemoth with a mirror finish, an electronic touchpad, and water and ice dispensers. It had two of those wiggly advert poppers stuck to the door – one boasting a frost-free capability and the other proclaiming that the mirror finish, remarkably, would not retain any fingerprints.

Now, at this point, you are probably asking yourself why I'm choosing to narrate my fridge-buying escapade in such detail, right? How is my experience of buying a fridge going to help you invest in yourself and create value in the corporate world? Well, there's a powerful metaphor in this story that will simply and effectively explain the concept of value, so bear with me.

As you would expect, the prices of the fridges increased the further along the row they were – the ones at the far end could demand a higher price because they were expected to create more value. This was for two reasons. The first was because their *functional* elements improved (could get colder; had more space; were frost free). The second was because of an *entirely additional set of elements* (more aesthetically pleasing; more reputable brands; longer warranties). In fact, it was clear that while the functional elements improved incrementally, the other elements improved exponentially – which is the reason why Mr Shiny Transformer-looking fridge at the end of the row cost almost ten times more than the one I bought, despite it being nowhere close to ten times more functional!

I have found this principle to be true in corporate environments as well: your ability to create value is a product of your functional abilities but also a function of a large set of other skills and attributes (your principles, communication skills, empathy and much more), and you need to develop and invest in both to succeed. Broadly speaking, the former abilities relate to your technical skillset and your ability to complete the fundamental and routine tasks of the job, while the latter abilities guide the way in which you work and the manner in which you navigate the social ecosystem of the corporate world. Of course, I am oversimplifying things here for the sake of the explanation (there are lots of other ways to categorize elements of value), but this serves my purpose in allowing me to explain the point.

Functional skills are table stakes – they are the essential prerequisites that you (and everyone else) need to land an interview and get in the door. If you cannot perform the technical aspect of the job, you simply cannot get by. But for you to distinguish yourself from your peers and progress to the very top, it is imperative that you focus on developing a whole host of other skills as well. In fact, the higher up the corporate ladder you go, the greater the emphasis on your ability to create value through non-technical skills. This is something most people often overlook, especially when they are starting out, which is one of the main reasons most don't make it to the top.

But before we can build non-technical skills, we must, of course, first build a very solid foundation set of technical, functional skills. Matt will take us through a very cool framework, which contains all of the building blocks for these skills – the education choices and decisions you make.

A FRAMEWORK FOR EDUCATIONAL DECISION-MAKING
- MATT

After reading *Chapter 2*, I'm sure you're not surprised that it's me writing a sub-section with the word 'framework' in it. Let's be honest: there is a lot of information out there about tertiary education – so much so that it sometimes seems impossible to decide what to do. We came up with a framework to help you navigate the educational opportunities ahead of you (see *Figure 1*).

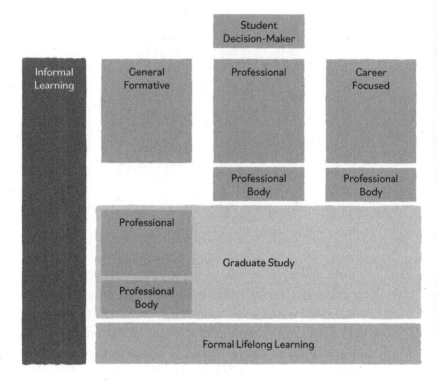

FIGURE 1
A SIMPLE FRAMEWORK FOR EDUCATIONAL DECISION-MAKING

Let's start by discussing the three main high-level educational options you'll have in front of you (outside of informal learning) if you are close to or have just finished high school (for those that are in or have completed university, or are already in a job, hang tight, we cover your options further on). The biggest choice you'll have is between pursuing a general formative (academic) education, a professional qualification or a career-focused qualification (I'll give examples of each). In many countries there are separate sets of academic institutions (and accrediting authorities) catering for each of these. There is also some overlap, which muddies the water. Many people start with a general academic degree and then top that up with a professional or more career-focused qualification. It all depends, of course, on how much time you think you can afford to spend at university.

The three options have different purposes. Let's start by looking, with broad brushstrokes and initially in general terms, at how learning pathways differ in their intended outcomes and focuses. We'll then look at how these principles apply to the three pathways.

If you were designing the training programme for plumbers, your purpose would be to produce someone who was highly efficient and competent at doing the job. You might include some specific principles about water levels and pressures, and the physical properties of different materials, but it wouldn't be appropriate or necessary to include a whole course in physics. A significant proportion of the training would focus on how to do things and there would be a lot of practical activity. So, a good training programme in this field would place the emphasis on what we call procedural knowledge, with a few specific principles included. The focus here would be on *how* to do things. The outcome would be to make things work.

The purpose of a programme for astrophysicists, on the other hand, would be to produce scientists who can extend our knowledge of the nature and composition of astronomical objects in the universe, such as stars and planets, by applying the theories and principles of physics and chemistry to the study of these objects. Education in this field would place a massive emphasis on the learning and development of theories and principles, but it would also include some procedural knowledge, which would be acquired through practical work in laboratories. The focus here would be on *what* and *why* things are as they are, and why they behave in a particular way. The outcome would be an explanation or deeper understanding.

The point I'm trying to illustrate is that in programmes associated with the three learning pathways described earlier, you will find a combination of the teaching of both principles and procedures appropriate to the field, but the *proportions* of each will vary according to the purpose of the programme.

We might expect, therefore, that career-focused programmes would have a larger component of procedural knowledge than theoretical knowledge. Many management programmes fall into the career-focused pathway. They include fields such as HR and people management, hospitality and tourism management, business management and public relations. Competent, proficient graduates in these fields need to go into the marketplace with high levels of 'how to' knowledge.

In professional fields, however, such as engineering, law, accounting, social work, teaching and medicine, while procedural knowledge is absolutely critical, it has to be underpinned by the theories and principles that are taught in some of the general disciplines relevant to these fields, such as physics and mathematics for engineering, jurisprudence for law, and anatomy and physiology for medicine.

And finally, it's these disciplines that predominate in general formative programmes. The emphasis is on theories and principles, as taught in subjects such as psychology, sociology, economics, political science,

literary and historical studies, geography and environmental studies, zoology, botany and chemistry... the
list goes on and on! But, even in these subjects, you will
always find elements of procedural knowledge as well.
The difference is in the mix.

SURVEY
– MATT

So, what does this mean in practical terms for you as a learner? How should you navigate the choppy waters of your educational investment decision to land the best position for yourself in the corporate world? The more I spoke to people about this, the more I realized the answers would be nuanced. So, Yusuf and I did something we love doing – we constructed a survey to help us answer some questions on this topic. We then turned to our network of professionals to help us find out which educational decisions work best for corporate success.

As an economist, I am obliged to state that we cannot say anything definitive about cause and effect here. Furthermore, we can't even extrapolate the findings to say they represent the corporate world as a whole. What we can say is that around 50 people in our professional network took part in a pretty comprehensive survey in which we asked them to make some trade-offs. Based on the comments made in the survey and messages we received, we know the respondents included multiple partners and directors at the big audit and consulting houses, as well as at the big law firms and banks. They also included lower and mid-level professionals with titles such as 'consultant,' 'investment professional,' 'talent manager' and 'senior associate.' We found the results surprising in some instances, but when we reflected on them, we realized there were interesting narratives to share. Let's get stuck in.

SURVEY RESULTS
PART I
– MATT

THE IMPACT OF
EDUCATIONAL DECISIONS
ON CAREERS

We started with two simple questions to get the ball rolling (see *Figure 2*). Firstly, we asked people in our corporate network if they thought that the educational decisions learners make at the end of high school have a significant impact on their corporate life outcomes (e.g. earning potential), and 97% said yes! We were pretty grateful for that result or we wouldn't have had very much more to write about in this chapter. Concerning the small share who said no, my guess is that this is because there are some successful people in organizations who navigate a very different route. It's possible – it's just a lot harder.

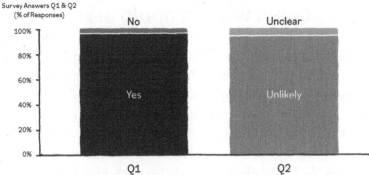

FIGURE 2
IMPORTANCE OF EDUCATIONAL DECISIONS AND
INFORMATION AVAILABILITY

HAVING THE RIGHT INFORMATION BEFORE MAKING THE EDUCATIONAL DECISION

The second question we asked was whether the people in our corporate network thought learners (at the end of high school or even in their early working years) have the right information to make optimal educational investment decisions for themselves. The overwhelming majority said they thought this was unlikely, and a small set thought it was unclear. Nobody thought it was likely that learners would have all the relevant information presented in a simple way to help them. If you are reading this and you're at the end of high school, our colleagues are saying you don't know it all and you should probably take the extra time to think about your next steps. Luckily, we also asked them their opinions about what those next steps should be.

GOING WIDE VS GOING DEEP

This brings us to the very important third question in our survey. We found the results of this one quite surprising, considering that the respondents were part of a corporate network and not an academic one. So, what did we ask? Well, we started by making a distinction (which, by the way, is linked to the framework in *Figure 1*). The distinction was between picking a degree in which you specialize early (e.g. an undergraduate LLB, or bachelor of laws) and starting work sooner, or beginning with a degree that is broader (e.g. a general bachelor's degree) and then moving on to an academic specialization. We asked, broadly, which route would lead to a more successful career in the corporate world (see *Figure 3*).

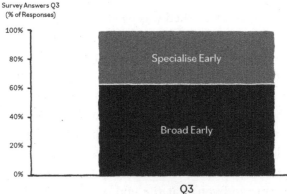

FIGURE 3

INVESTING IN BROAD OR SPECIALIZED EDUCATION EARLY ON

About 65% of the respondents believed that doing a broader degree earlier on was a better choice, while 35% thought it would be better (all else being equal) to specialize straight after high school. I want to make some observations in relation to this outcome.

The first point to make is that the results reflect the fact that this issue isn't even fully resolved in the minds of academics or corporates[7] – and, relatedly, school counsellors sometimes struggle to give advice on this topic because the answer isn't obvious or simple.[8] If you are very sure of what you want to do, you might feel you want to make a bet on that by picking a speciality early. I would, however, warn against rushing into such a decision – especially if you are being influenced by your parents. Keep in mind that many parents are anxious about the employment opportunities facing their children (you) after studying. This anxiety, attached to real economic constraints (university is expensive), means you are likely to be pushed to choose a programme that is tightly focused on a particular career or profession. That said, there is nothing fundamentally wrong with this, and the cost of university is a further argument for picking a speciality early to minimize your study time. And, as you can see from the survey results, there was still a significant share of our network that thought specializing early was the right choice for corporate success.

My personal experience is that if you've had the chance to do a broad degree followed by an academic specialization, you will have a slower career trajectory for the first five to ten years (you may, for example, start working three years after your early-specialized peers). However, as you move closer to the top of a large company, your chances of getting onto the executive committee (or becoming the CEO) will be higher because of your broader academic background. The broader academic foundation will most likely help you to apply general principles to solve problems across a wider range of contexts, as opposed to a set of procedural solutions, which may be appropriate to only a limited number of situations. What do I mean by this? A broader general qualification may give you the advantage of greater conceptual and analytical sophistication than a more tightly focused course of study is likely to do. The complexity of decision-making at the top is so high that purely professional qualifications might leave you less well equipped than you hoped. I must also admit that this is a contestable position, and one that many will disagree with. But with all of my educational and corporate experience and based on all the conversations I've had with senior business leaders as well as academics, it's the position I stand by today. Sadly, and this really is sadly, this route is more expensive – both from a purely financial perspective (more years of university fees) and from an opportunity cost perspective (fewer years working in the early days).

A further, but related, point relates to the concept of VUCA (volatility, uncertainty, complexity and ambiguity). I'm writing this in the middle of the Covid-19 pandemic. Even before this period, there were emerging narratives around VUCA and the need for learners to be equipped with '21st-century skills.'[9] In my opinion, there is a lot of silly hand-waving and abuse of this language in corporate discourse (let me refrain from a rant here). The most important thing for you to realize, in your decision-making, is that the rate at which the world is changing is higher than it has ever been before.[10] This means that things are continually changing and the level of complexity is extreme. As a result, there will be an increasing premium on people who have excellent backgrounds in 'principles' and not just 'procedures.' Having the capacity to think creatively, to apply ideas differently and to innovate is the name of the game.

Here is an over-simplified example to make the distinction. There is a ton of good that comes from studying to be a chartered accountant – but imagine we end up living in a world where either of two things happen. The first possibility is that some smart kid sitting in their bedroom at home invents a completely different set of accounting rules and standards that is just way better than the ones we have today and corporates decide to implement them. The second is that we finally start better leveraging AI and all of the accounting manual checks and balances you've spent years learning suddenly get done by a machine. My point isn't that becoming a chartered accountant is bad – rather, if you haven't invested in acquiring a broader set of principles (e.g. around problem-solving, logic and ethics), then you will, quite unfortunately, become redundant. I've always teased chartered accountant friends of mine about that specialization, although it's mostly because I remain jealous of their ability to quickly understand the financial position of a business. Nevertheless, it remains true (though this may change) that many (and I mean very many) CEOs of large successful businesses are chartered accountants.[11]

CHOICE OF GENERAL DEGREE

Next, we asked our respondents to imagine someone was going down the general route. What type of general bachelor's degree would they recommend to prepare someone for a corporate career? *Figure 4* shows their responses.

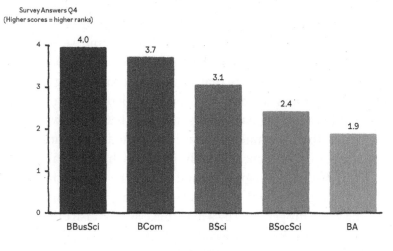

Survey Answers Q4
(Higher scores = higher ranks)

FIGURE 4
PERCEIVED DEGREE TYPE RELEVANCE

Higher scores mean respondents ranked a degree as better for a broad start to a corporate career. The respondents said the top two broad degrees were the Bachelor of Business Science (BBusSci) and the Bachelor of Commerce (BCom). These two were followed by a Bachelor of Science (BSci), a Bachelor of Social Science (BSocSci) and a Bachelor of Arts (BA).

Two things are interesting here. Firstly, as you may have expected, the BBusSci and the BCom received a lot of support as good broad foundation degrees for a career in the corporate world (sorry, Matt, no Nobel Prize for that finding). But, secondly, it is interesting to see the score for the good old BA. Yes, it's the lowest score, but it's not as low as I anticipated. When I looked at the data more deeply, I found that around 15% of the respondents ranked the BA in first or second place. There is an important insight here. Assuming you have the ability to specialize down the line, the BA can actually offer an incredible foundation for a corporate career. Keep that in mind!

CHOICE OF SPECIALIST DEGREE OR QUALIFICATION

The next question touches on a much-blogged-about topic: the choice between a master's degree other than an MBA, an MBA itself, qualification as a chartered accountant (CA) or qualification as a chartered financial analyst (CFA). For some reason, everyone has an opinion on this one. My perspective is that the truth is quite simple and boring:

- Becoming a **CA** is good if you want to be an accountant for a long time (not necessarily forever)
- Becoming a **CFA** is good if you want to be an investment professional
- Getting an **MBA** is a good way to better understand the business world if you haven't got an understanding already (some MBAs go seriously deep on complex business topics, including finance)
- Getting **another master's degree** is good *if* you are passionate about it and *if* you believe it has applications in a corporate environment

Our respondents ranked these more specialized options in our survey (see *Figure 5*). We recognized that this wasn't really a fair question, as the decision heavily hinges on your ultimate goal or purpose. Nonetheless, people like comparing things, even when it's inappropriate, and we couldn't resist the temptation.

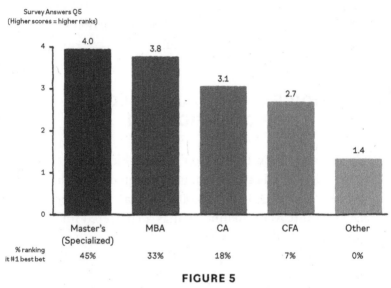

FIGURE 5
PERCEIVED VALUE OF TYPE OF POSTGRADUATE
STUDY TITLE

Despite the slightly dodgy nature of the question itself, there were some interesting results. It's clear our respondents placed a premium on having a master's degree (either an MBA or another type). It's also clear that the CA and CFA received similar levels of support, although the CA received slightly more – probably reflecting its somewhat broader application (as opposed to a CFA, which is highly specialized).

But why did the non-MBA master's degree get the most support? There are two potential reasons. Firstly, there are increasing demands for experts who also have broad academic backgrounds in the corporate labour market – these could be economists, data scientists or other technical experts. That's the interpretation I like, because I have a master's degree in economics. But the second reason might actually be because of the way the question was framed. MBA, CA and CFA are all very specific programmes. If we had separated out the various non-MBA master's options, it would have split the votes. But because this was a catch-all option, it had the benefit of drawing all the votes of people who preferred a master's in one of the many other areas – data science, economics, law, finance and so on. There's a learning point in all of this: be very careful when you're interpreting survey data responses. Context and framing matter! Luckily for you, I understand data and surveys, and I'm a pretty honest guy.

SURVEY RESULTS
PART II
- YUSUF

TO DOCTOR OR
NOT TO DOCTOR,
THAT IS THE QUESTION
- YUSUF

An assessment of tertiary studies would not be complete without a perspective on a doctoral degree, so we asked the respondents whether they believed that the improvement in career trajectory offered by a doctoral degree was commensurate with the amount of time and the financial investment it demands. As shown in *Figure 6*, 90% of the respondents felt that a doctoral degree isn't worth the time and money if your career is non-academic – the juice simply isn't worth the squeeze.

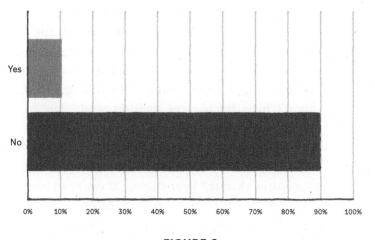

FIGURE 6
IS A DOCTORAL DEGREE WORTH THE INVESTMENT
FOR A NON-ACADEMIC CAREER?

There are some other interesting insights that we derived from this result, especially in the context of some of our earlier findings.

Firstly, it's worth clarifying that while the respondents felt a doctoral degree has limited value in non-academic sectors, they also thought that specialized post-graduate study is important – but only up to a master's level. In part, this outcome is probably related to opportunity cost – the respondents most likely felt that there are other, more productive ways of investing your time and money to improve the trajectory of your career (some of which we discuss in other chapters of this book).

On another level, this result echoes the outcome of the question about going wide versus going deep (see *Figure 3*) – the respondents placed a premium on people who have excellent academic backgrounds with an emphasis on principles and less so on procedures. Again, there is certainly value placed on specialization and deep expertise in an area. However, when these are acquired at the expense of developing a broader knowledge base and conceptual understanding, it *can* (but doesn't have to) become counter-productive to your holistic development, and ultimately to the trajectory of your career.

It's also important to consider the longevity of any skillset acquired through your studies. If you're an academic, your job is to stay abreast of the latest research and developments within your area of specialization to ensure that your knowledge and expertise remain relevant and up to date. This can be challenging within the dynamic corporate landscape. The risk here is that your skills could become outdated quickly, especially given the rapidly changing landscape exacerbated by factors like VUCA and Covid-19. Given these considerations, your personal circumstances will play an important role in determining whether further studies justify the opportunity cost of not engaging in other activities that contribute to your skill development.

IMPORTANCE OF GRADES, INSTITUTION AND TYPE OF DEGREE

We then asked the respondents to rank three factors in terms of importance for the career trajectory of a learner: the type of degree completed, the grades achieved and the perceived prestige of the university. University prestige came in as the most important, followed by the type of degree and then the grades achieved (see *Figure 7*). But the votes were so equally distributed that the rankings were actually very close to each other, which essentially means that all of these factors matter. Let's dive a bit deeper into each factor to understand why this is the case.

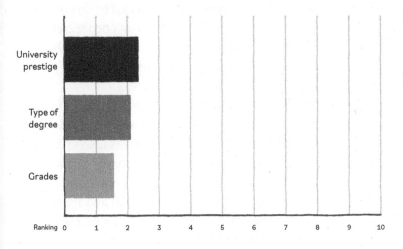

FIGURE 7
TYPE OF DEGREE, GRADES AND UNIVERSITY
PRESTIGE RANKED BY IMPORTANCE

There are at least four potential reasons that university prestige came in as the most important factor (albeit only by a slim margin). First, content and curriculum vary between universities, despite the qualifications being the same, and some institutions maintain higher standards and demand very high amounts of academic rigour (effort) in order for students to do well on assessments. Second, some institutions have superior facilities and especially highly qualified and renowned faculty members (professors and lecturers), both of which contribute significantly to the knowledge and skill level that learners acquire. Third, the stringent admission requirements of some universities result in high-achieving learners making up the majority of the students who gain entry to the institution, which has a positive impact on the overall learning experience and the development of all students. Fourth, the networking opportunities provided by certain universities cannot be underestimated. It's an open secret that prestigious institutions often attract individuals from affluent, influential backgrounds, and the value of a strong network is hard to overstate.

As a side note, the reality is that there are students from a whole range of different backgrounds who do not get to access the best universities. Cost is often the greatest barrier to entry (although if you do really well in school and are from a disadvantaged background, there are many scholarships out there that you can and must apply for). The best advice that we can give you is that you should direct your efforts towards getting into the best university that your circumstances allow.

The type of degree you study came in as a close second to the reputation of the university you attend in terms of importance for your career trajectory. This result reinforces the insights gained from prior questions about choosing between specialized and general degrees. It underscores the importance of making informed decisions early on about the academic path you intend to follow.

Grades ranked the lowest of the three factors. It's important to clarify that this doesn't mean the respondents felt that good grades are not important; rather, when considered in the context of the university you attend and the type of degree you choose to study, they were considered the least important factor – though by a small margin. The short story is that grades *do* matter, a lot, and you must focus on shooting the lights out here because this is the area you have most control over. There are more people with degrees today than there ever have been, and this is a trend that is unlikely to change in the near future. The job market is painfully competitive, and if you are not able to distinguish yourself by having a degree from a prestigious university, the only other way you are going to get ahead of other applicants is through your grades. So, put in your best effort and work your butt off to get the best grades you can, regardless of where you study or what you study! This may sound like conventional advice, but I would be remiss if I did not make a special point of expressing the importance of good grades in a chapter dedicated to investing into yourself. Remember, your academic record will follow you throughout your career and may very well be a material factor in deciding whether you will land that dream job a good few years down the track.

But the value of good grades extends beyond the classroom. Earning them teaches you to acquire the habits of hard work and aim high early on. Moreover, good grades can open doors to opportunities like scholarships and accolades, enhancing the impact of your CV in ways you might not have envisioned.

ONLINE LEARNING

It's impossible to ignore the impact that virtual studies and online courses are having on the way we build functional skills. Today, you can access short courses called MOOCS (massive open online courses) from some of the best universities in the world – many of them free of charge! The argument for this type of study is compelling and must be seriously considered. So, we asked our respondents a question directly related to online learning and its place in the world of educating and skilling a learner. The outcome, despite all the noise surrounding virtual studies (which has been amplified by the Covid-19 situation), was that 80% of the respondents felt that online education was an emerging trend that would *not* replace traditional tertiary education (see *Figure 8*).

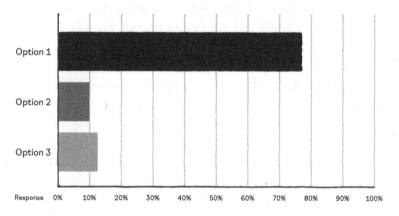

Option 1:   I think it's an emerging trend but it won't replace traditional tertiary education
– it's more relevant to lifelong learning

Option 2:   I think that traditinoal face-to-face education will fall away and everything will be online

Option 3:   I think most online learning is poor quality and it is very unlikely to achieve improved educational outcomes for learners

FIGURE 8
WILL ONLINE LEARNING REPLACE TRADITIONAL
TERTIARY EDUCATION?

I think it's safe to say that this was an expected outcome. I, like the majority of the respondents, believe that traditional learning still matters and that online learning in its current construct is best suited to continuous learning because it is an efficient means for working professionals to refresh or 'top up' their functional skills and understanding of a subject that they studied at university, often many years earlier. I encourage you to use online courses to augment and complement your university studies. This will enhance your knowledge, enrich your understanding, and showcase your initiative and willingness to go the extra mile – qualities that will undoubtedly contribute positively to your profile.

GENERALIZED SKILLS & COMPETENCIES

Beyond the subject matter knowledge and technical skills that a learner will acquire (and hopefully retain) through tertiary studies, we asked the respondents to provide us with a single, attribute, ability or trait that they felt it was important for learners to develop more generally to improve their career trajectory. *Figure 9* shows the results (larger words were mentioned more commonly).

FIGURE 9

THE MOST IMPORTANT CORE SKILL

It was clear that the respondents felt that the Four Cs – critical thinking, communication, collaboration and creativity – are important additional competencies to develop as well.

Critical thinking is the objective analysis and evaluation of an issue to form a judgement. You will be exposed to many different theories, models and frameworks for analysis throughout your tertiary studies. These are tools that are used repeatedly to assess and analyse data and information, to synthesize insights and to help solve problems. This process will teach you *how to think* objectively about a problem and how to structure an informed solution (i.e. decide on the best course of action) within a given set of circumstances. In some fields it will also refer to the ability to look beyond the face value of what is presented, identify the shortcomings of a position or argument, and explore alternative perspectives.

Collaboration is the action of working with people to produce something. You will engage with many different people at university, most of whom you will be meeting for the first time. You will be expected to form small groups and work together on a regular basis to produce pieces of work. Through this process, you will learn how to work and engage effectively with people who have different personalities, ways of thinking and areas of expertise, and also learn how to manage team dynamics, both as a leader and as a participant or team member.

Communication means imparting or exchanging information through speaking, writing or some other medium. You can have the best ideas in the world, but if you are unable to communicate them effectively, they are of no value to anyone. The assessment process at a tertiary level requires you to consume lots of information and synthesize insights. You will need to communicate clearly and succinctly by writing essays, taking tests and exams, making presentations, and participating in class discussions and debates.

Creativity is the use of original ideas to create something. I never considered myself to be a creative person because I thought, rather foolishly, that creative people were born, not made, and were good at things like art – something that was never a strong point for me. At university, however, I was enlightened to the fact that this was not entirely true – creativity covers a broad spectrum of activities (not just art!) and is a skill that can be developed. The nature of the assessments forced me to provide innovative and imaginative solutions to problems, and I grew progressively better through repetition. So, I would say that a better definition of creativity is the ability to propose an innovative solution to a problem, often by taking your existing knowledge and combining elements, or applying it in new ways.

The importance of cultivating these Four C's cannot be overstated. These are timeless competencies that will serve you well at every stage of your career (and life more broadly).

PERSONAL SKILLS

Remember the transformer-looking fridge in my fridge-purchasing escapade? The one that cost ten times more than the one I bought, despite being only incrementally more functional, because it had an additional set of softer, intangible value elements? Well, our respondents felt that there are some similar elements that are important for your career trajectory. Let's call them personal skills. These are the attitudes, behaviours and mindsets that make up your professional identity, which differentiates you by influencing the way you work and engage with people. I believe these personal skills become more important – more than your functional skills – as your career progresses. We gave out respondents space to tell us what they thought were important personal skills, and we categorized the responses we received into four key areas.

The first is **physical appearance**. There are some aspects of your physiological make-up that you cannot change. What matters is being able to make the most of what you have. There has been a significant shift in professional attire over past decade or so, with most organizations relaxing their dress code and allowing people to express their own individual sense of style and their personality. However, there are some definite ground rules: neatness, freshness and cleanliness, always! Let me assure you that most people do in fact judge a book by its cover, so make sure that your physical appearance creates a positive perception about you.

The second is **mental toughness**. At the outset of your career, you are probably going to be overwhelmed with the amount of work you are going to have to do and horrified by the lack of assistance and support you will get (you have been warned!). Deadlines will be tight, and clients and your superiors will be demanding. You are going to have to learn to deal with insane amounts of pressure, anxiety and uncertainty, and the only way you will be able to manage it all is by learning to be mentally strong and resilient.

The third is **emotional intelligence**, which is defined as the ability to perceive, evaluate and respond to your emotions and the emotions of others. Essentially, this means treating people empathetically, considering why they feel and act the way they do, and trying to see things from their perspective. It's about treating them with kindness and respect. It also means managing your own emotions so that they don't drive you to act in a way that you would regret. Remember, you are going to be working with people, and having a high level of emotional intelligence – specifically, being able understand and deal with the complexities of human behaviour – will enable you to build lasting relationships and networks (we've dedicated a whole chapter to this because it is so important; see *Chapter 5*).

The fourth is **optimism**. People are drawn to people who are optimistic and have a positive outlook. You, like every other person, are going to go through some very hard times and will encounter some really difficult people along the way (another topic to which we have dedicated a whole chapter; see *Chapter 6*). Your ability to remain optimistic and positive will contribute significantly to your ability to overcome those challenges.

DURATION OF EDUCATION

To end the survey, we wanted to ascertain the sweet spot for the number of years that should be spent undertaking tertiary studies. Thankfully, the average of the responses ties in perfectly with our earlier findings (big sigh of relief here!). See *Figure 10* for the results.

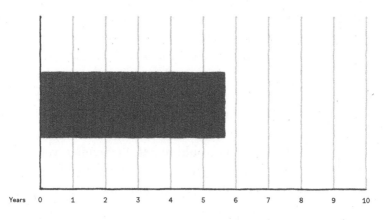

FIGURE 10
THE MOST IMPORTANT CORE SKILL

The respondents felt that five or six years is the amount of time that should be spent in tertiary studies, which is roughly the amount of time it would take to get a bachelor's and then a master's level degree (of course, this assumes that you don't repeat any years). Now, this may seem a long time, especially when you're coming out of 12 years of schooling and are raring to get out into the working world and start earning your loot. But take it from someone who has been there and done that – don't be in a hurry. Your years at university will probably be some of the most enjoyable of your life, so appreciate them and take the time to build a solid skill set. Arm yourself with an appropriate level of expertise within your subject area and soak up the experience that will undoubtedly shape you as a person (hopefully positively!) before venturing out into the working world.

CHAPTER 4

BECOME AN EXPERT

BY YUSUF

I'll never forget my first day of work. There I was, well overdressed in a suit for my role as a creditors clerk (something akin to a 'financial analyst'), with my heart pumping and adrenaline racing. I was nervous and stealthily wiped my sweaty palms on my trousers while I waited for someone from HR to collect me from reception.

Instead of the epic hero's parade that I'd deluded myself into expecting, my entrance into the office felt more like a short and direct walk to the gallows. I was met mostly with quizzical stares and a few sardonic smiles on the way to my corner. No, not the corner office, but an actual corner – my desk was literally in the corner at the back of the office.

Shortly after the HR team deserted me, I felt a thick, heavy hand on my shoulder. This guy (let's call him Frank) introduced himself as my manager and told me that before we got started with my training, he wanted to show me around the office. Frank actually meant that he wanted to show me where the kitchen was. And so, the first training I received in my corporate life was instructions on how to make Frank's coffee. My career had literally only just started and my hopes and dreams were beginning to wilt like warm lettuce.

This was not how I had expected this day to go. I had done reasonably well at university – not just academically, but as an all-rounder – so surely that confidence and success would naturally follow into my working life and people would afford me some recognition at the outset, right? Wrong! In a moment of absolute clarity amid my anguish while stirring Frank's coffee in the kitchen, I realized that I was now in a new world. I had graduated from the pond of university to the sea of corporate – a place filled with uncertainty, ambition and sharks – big ones! Yes, I had earned my right to be here, and had the baseline skills and knowledge I needed to survive for now (which was why I had got through the interview and been offered the job). But to succeed in this environment, I would need to do two very important things – become an expert at something and build a solid reputation for it. This is the focus of this chapter.

Time to suit up. Its game time.

THE EXPERT

HR processes and corporate culture have come a long way since my first day. Today, there are inductions to help you find your feet and extensive training and support to get you going in the job. There are also fancy coffee machines at most offices – some even boast on-site baristas (can you believe it!) – and there's a general perception that all employees expect to (and should) be treated with sensitivity and consideration.

The definition and characteristics of an expert have also changed. When I was starting out, I was introduced to the concept of the 'big sharp sword' – a metaphor for core competence, unique skills and deep expertise in an area. The professional world valued people who had a big sharp sword, and the 'generalist' who lacked extensive procedural knowledge was apparently destined to dabble their way to mediocrity.

The perception is quite different today. With the relentless advancement of technology, the rapid pace of change in the world and the extreme uncertainty we now face (exacerbated by Covid-19), there's a growing premium being placed on people who can do a few things well and problem solve by drawing from knowledge across a wide range of disciplines. Paradoxically, these individuals are called 'expert generalists.'[6] Perhaps the most significant insight that can be drawn from this label is that the world still values experts; what has changed, though, is that the spectrum of things to specialize in has expanded significantly. So, it is important to choose your area of specialization carefully in a world of near limitless choice and options. My advice is to let your passions and career goals steer your decision-making. The modern corporate landscape values those who integrate their skills with their aspirations. By aligning your specialty with what drives you, you're not only on course to mastering a field, but also to shaping a purpose-driven path.

Another consideration is the timing of your specialization. You may recall that 65% of our survey respondents believed that pursuing a general degree early on, rather than a specialized degree, would yield more promising future career prospects (see *Figure 3*). Personally, I agree with this view and believe going wide, as opposed to deep, early on is for most the better option. It's also important, today more than ever, to be agile and flexible. You need to have the ability to pivot yourself and apply your knowledge and skills across a broad set of problems and disciplines – more than you need to have deep procedural knowledge in one area only. But at some point, you are going to have to ask yourself a very important question: What do I want to be known for? This is going to require you to zone in and focus on a specific area and demonstrate your ability to consistently create unique and differentiated value in that space.

THE REPUTATION

Let's do a little experiment. I want you to say each of the following names out loud with a pause of five seconds between each name: Steve Jobs, Nelson Mandela, Serena Williams, Elon Musk. You must have spent the past 20 years on the Moon if these thoughts (in this order) did not come to mind: Apple, South African freedom fighter, the greatest female tennis player of all time, Tesla. Now do the exercise with people that you know personally and observe the thoughts that come to your mind.

The point of this exercise is to illustrate that we usually associate people with the things that they do or have done. The corporate world is no different. You will be judged by the things you have done and the results you produced, so you need to build a track record of achievements that will become synonymous with your professional identity. This is your reputation. You are absolutely right if you're thinking that a reputation is rooted in values and ethics (which is why we have dedicated an entire chapter to ethics; see *Chapter 7*). However, the things you have succeeded and failed at in a tangible, measurable sense make up a big portion of your reputation too. This becomes increasingly important as you progress further into your career. In fact, your reputation becomes more about what you have done and less about what you know or could potentially do as you progress.

Building a reputation takes time, effort and focus. It's one of the most important determinants of your corporate success. Yes, it's that big a deal. It's a process that is as much an art as it is a science, and it is mostly a function of your ability to consistently demonstrate expert-level knowledge, skill and experience *and* produce superior results. This is no easy feat, which is why this chapter brings you our collective experience and knowledge, and some contemporary wisdom too, to provide you with a plan for executing this mandate. Let's get stuck into some processes for becoming an expert and building a reputation.

HOW TO BECOME AN EXPERT

In 2008, Malcolm Gladwell published a book called *Outliers: The Story of Success*.[12] The book was a huge hit and contains many original and insightful ideas. But the absolute stand-out, in my opinion, is the provocative "10,000-hour rule."

Gladwell studied experts from across a number of disciplines and fields, including musicians, professional athletes and programmers, to understand how much practice time it took to become an 'expert' at something. He concluded that it took 10,000 hours of focused, dedicated practice to become an expert in an area. For a while, the 10,000-hour rule was all the rage, although not necessarily because it was true – it was just catchy and easy to remember. In fact, this theory has been debunked many times over the years and closer analysis revealed issues with both the research that Gladwell undertook and the conclusions he drew.

There are two things we can learn from this. Firstly, there is no proof that it takes 10,000 hours of practice to become an expert at anything (thankfully!). Secondly, there is no single clear path to becoming an expert because there are myriad specific factors and variables that every path presents. The only constant, as Gladwell outlines, is that becoming an expert requires depth and breadth in three core elements: specific knowledge, skills within the relevant area and experience in operating in that area.[13]

In *Chapter 3* we covered getting a degree (a tertiary education), which is the first meaningful step towards acquiring professional-level knowledge. But the knowledge you acquire through your degree is just your baseline. You will need to build on this base by continually expanding your understanding of the field or profession you pursue – the operative word in that sentence being *'continually.'* This is because becoming an expert is more of a journey than it is a destination.

Next I'm going to introduce two models to help articulate the expert journey. I can't stake a claim to either of them as they were both developed by other people, but I wanted to pay tribute to them by including them in this book because they have helped me tremendously along my own path. They are the *Dreyfus Model of Skill Acquisition* and the Japanese concept of *ikigai*, which is all about passion and purpose.

THE DREYFUS MODEL OF SKILL ACQUISITION

In 1980, Stuart E. Dreyfus and Hubert L. Dreyfus wrote a paper titled "A Five-Stage Model of the Mental Activities Involved in Direct Skill Acquisition," which essentially lays out five distinct phases that everyone must go through along their journey to becoming an expert (see *Figure 11*).[14] I've found this model useful as it is less of a prescriptive approach and more of a lens through which I have been able to assess my own progress along the journey towards becoming an expert.

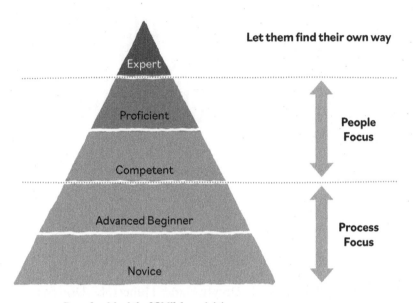

Dreyfus Model of Skill Acquisition

FIGURE 11
THE DREYFUS MODEL OF SKILL ACQUISITION

The model provides a mechanism through which you can assess the degree to which you possess desired skills and competencies. The five levels are as follows:

1. **Novice:** At this stage, you have little to no skills and experience of your own. You are unable operate outside the realm of the procedural knowledge and guidelines you have been provided with, and you cannot complete the tasks at hand without guidance and supervision.

2. **Advanced beginner:** You have gained sufficient skills and experience to have a set of baseline capabilities that you can apply to new situations unsupervised.

3. **Competent:** You take a more holistic approach to dealing with situations and begin to explore ways of using your own experience and skills. This leads to more proactive and considered approaches to future situations.
4. **Proficient:** At this stage you choose the appropriate solutions to problems. You have essentially transitioned from applying rules to considering situations. You perform well in dynamic and undefined situations and are able to provide guidance and support to others.
5. **Expert:** You are able to see the entire spectrum of a situation while understanding its idiosyncrasies and nuances. You are able to act intuitively with a deep sense of conviction in all that you do. You set out plans and courses of action for others while continually refining and updating your own skills and capabilities.

Now, let's review some considerations for moving through each stage.

NOVICE TO ADVANCED BEGINNER: OBSERVE, LISTEN AND TAKE NOTES

One of the most underrated skills is the simple act of observation – watching with focus and concentration to see what people do and how they do it. The key point at this stage is to register and absorb as much information as possible, and then make notes of the new information you have gained. Become a sponge and put yourself out there in as many ways as possible to maximize your reach and your ability to access as much knowledge as possible, while diligently applying the procedural knowledge set out for you to complete the tasks at hand.

ADVANCED BEGINNER TO COMPETENT: EXPERIMENT AND PRACTISE

Once you have a baseline set of skills and experience and are armed with an arsenal of information gained through observing the various situations you have exposed yourself to, it's time to practise by applying your knowledge to new situations. This will require you to identify problems and situations that are unfamiliar and test your ability to achieve the desired outcome. Naturally, you will sometimes fail – miserably at times – but that is what you are meant to do at this stage. You *should* be making mistakes, learning from those mistakes and repeating this process ad nauseam until you understand and have substantial confidence in your procedural knowledge within your desired field of expertise.

COMPETENT TO PROFICIENT: ENGAGE AND GUIDE

The most significant aspect of competency and proficiency is your ability to see the big picture (in other words, make an impact at a macro level) and guide others to perform their tasks better. I have found that the best way to do this is to act as a mentor to others and get involved in managing and guiding them. This provides an opportunity to not just apply your skills and experience but also learn through the dynamic process of working with others. This can be valuable in helping you to reassess and refine aspects of your skill set, ensuring they remain relevant.

PROFICIENT TO EXPERT: REFINE AND LEAD

Develop a rich understanding of your industry and the social, political and economic factors that influence it by engaging with news and other media. Register for online courses to help you stay relevant and abreast of the latest developments in your field. Attend conferences to get a sense of what is happening from leaders and other experts. Write and publish thought-leadership pieces. Find and reach out to people who are doing big things in your field and try to get some time to chat to them. They may not always respond to your request, but you have nothing to lose by trying. The purpose of this 'knowledge-stacking' process is to build a deep and intimate understanding of your area of expertise, and understand the trends, challenges and opportunities – and where they are headed in the future.

THE HIGH-LEVEL VIEW

Every job or profession has its own set of technical skills that you need to possess in order to perform the required tasks. Some are very specific (e.g. removing a brain tumour) and some more generic (e.g. building a financial model or a PowerPoint presentation). An expert generalist, as an example, must be able to link pieces of information from many different fields and distil insights that can be used to solve a problem. Whatever the relevant skills may be, you need to identify and prioritize them. According to the Pareto principle (also known as the 80/20) rule, 20% of the technical skills will enable you to do 80% of the job.[15] Find that 20% and dedicate time and effort to really honing and mastering those skills.

To be recognized as possessing expert-level skill, you will need to do three things. Firstly, your skills must lead to performance that is consistently superior to that of your peers. Secondly, your expertise must produce real, tangible results. You will be pleased to know that despite there being a range of theories on how much practice it takes to become an expert, there is one important point of agreement – experts are not born, they are made. Through dedication and quality practice, you absolutely have the potential to develop the expert-level skills you desire.

Finally, you need experience – the importance of which cannot be overstated. This is time spent applying your knowledge and skills in a live, real environment, navigating the challenges and complexities of the job that needs to be done. The trick is not only to get as much experience as you can, but also to expand your breadth of experience across other areas that are related to or are influenced by the area that you have chosen to specialize in, especially early on in your career. As Stuart and Hubert Dreyfus suggest, as proficiency grows, reliance on abstract principles diminishes in favor of concrete experience. As you begin this journey, remember that progressing from novice to expert relies on the fusion of dedicated practice and the nuanced wisdom of hands-on involvement.[16]

SUSTAINING THE EXPERT PURSUIT

So you need to build a knowledge base and a craft, hone your skills and acquire extensive experience to become an expert. But how do you sustain this pursuit and stay motivated over the long term? In my opinion, there are two things that are essential to sustaining your pursuit of becoming an expert and having the reputation to go with it.

Firstly, you must cultivate a deep sense of curiosity. Steve Jobs has been described as having an insatiable curiosity and would ask questions that constantly challenged the status quo.[17] Colleagues and associates who knew Jobs attest to the fact that his knack for asking thought-provoking questions significantly contributed to his success.

It takes confidence to ask questions, especially tough ones that may challenge norms and traditional ways of thinking and doing things. I encourage you to have the confidence to ask those questions, often, so that you can learn, grow and develop. However, a note of caution:

moderation is key. As you step into the corporate realm, it's crucial to strike a balance between inquisitiveness and humility. It is very important to create the right impression, especially when you are starting out. If you enter the corporate arena overly confident, questioning everything or presuming to have all the answers, you are simply going to piss people off. This inevitably is going to impact people's willingness to work with you, potentially setting you up for failure. You need to be humble enough to understand that you are in a new world. Keep your focus on knowledge acquisition, skill development, and experience accumulation and empower yourself to be curious to ask questions. In doing this, you will earn your right to exude confidence, ultimately commanding respect through the tangible results you achieve.

IKIGAI

The next thing you need to do to sustain your pursuit of becoming an expert is to find purpose and enjoyment in your work. It's about aligning your area of expertise with your intrinsic interests and maintaining a high level of engagement. Take it from me, this isn't as straightforward as it might seem. I spent the better part of my twenties in search of purpose and without a proper plan in place. The result was far too much time spent disillusioned and unproductive. Only much later was I introduced to a model that helped me to articulate a purpose and sustain my pursuit of becoming an expert.

This brings us to the second major model considered in this chapter, popularized by Héctor García and Francesc Miralles, authors of the book *Ikigai: The Japanese Secret to a Long and Happy Life*.[18] *Ikigai* is a Japanese concept that strives to balance the spiritual with the practical. This balance is found at the intersection of where your passions and talents converge with the things that the world needs and is willing to pay you for (see *Figure 12*). This may sound wishy-washy and a bit out of place in this chapter (and possibly this book), but I can assure you it has a very useful and practical application and can help you to discover your professional sweet spot – the path, field or discipline that you want to become an expert in.

FIGURE 12
THE *IKIGAI* DIAGRAM

The diagram is self-explanatory and I'm not going to go into a whole lot of detail explaining each of the four quadrants. I will just impress upon you the importance of using it to find your own *ikigai* because every truly great expert finds purpose and enjoyment in their work, and you are no different.

Just a tip: don't expect to find your *ikigai* early on. Expect to spend a decent chunk of time grinding away on painful projects with painful people and being disgustingly underpaid for the soul that you are selling, and yes, you will probably want to quit, many times. Don't worry, we've all been, and rest assured, it won't last forever! It is a challenging but necessary part of your path towards becoming an expert. But what would be truly sad would be if that process continued indefinitely – it would be unsustainable. By adopting the *ikigai* perspective for your career, you can shape some of your decisions and steer your trajectory towards purpose, significance, enjoyment and gratification. I, for one, have managed to do just that.

EARNING SOCIAL CREDIT

A final important topic relevant to developing expertise is social credit. Remember, you are not just attempting to become an expert. You want to build a reputation so that you become known and desirable in the corporate world for the value you can create. You want to get to a point where when people think about you, they associate your expertise and the results you have produced in an area with you as an individual.

Part of building that reputation requires you to showcase your abilities to the right people. However, make no mistake – excellent work will always speak for itself. If you have produced great work, the right people will very likely come to know about it. So, for the most part, let your work and results speak for themselves. Don't be the obnoxious person who makes sure everyone in the office knows they helped the company to save a negligible amount of money. Nobody likes that person and I can assure you, they are going nowhere fast.

But balance is important. You don't want to be cooped up in the corner (like I was) churning out stellar work without anyone knowing your name. Get out and start connecting with people. Offer to help others with pieces of work so that you can showcase your skills and abilities. Senior people are always looking for junior people who will make them look good. If you can demonstrate your ability to add value, you will kill two birds with one stone – you will make important contacts and connections who will act as leverage points for you to meet other important people. Moreover, you will likely secure yourself a mentor who will provide you with some level of tutelage and guidance in the form of trademark wisdom from their own experience. This could significantly help you along your path. That said, don't lose sight of your core responsibilities and tasks by allowing ambition to get in the way of consistently delivering value in the job that you are paid to do. Remember the Pareto principle: 80% of your time and focus needs to be here, but keep that 20% on the lookout for other types of work too.

Before we conclude this chapter, let me share a final nugget of wisdom for becoming an expert and building a sterling reputation: embed yourself within the professional community of your field. Maintain a robust link to the pulse of your organization and its broader context. Stay attuned to the ever-evolving landscape and cultivate connections. Hopefully before long, with dedication and focused effort, you can become a really big fish (or shark if you choose) in the sea of your corporate profession. The next chapter considers building a network in more depth.

CHAPTER 5

DEVELOP A NETWORK

BY YUSUF

Bill Gates is among the most famous and successful people in the world. He will probably go down in history as the pioneer of the personal computing revolution of the 1980s and as the founder of a company – Microsoft – that changed the face of humanity forever.

Most of his story is well known: a college dropout with an obsessive work ethic, relentless ambition and a passion for writing software code. Oh and let's not forget he also held the spot as the richest man on the planet for a long time. But there's an important nuance in his story that is less well known and that is arguably the reason for his and Microsoft's astronomical success.

As Robert Cringely reports in *Accidental Empires*, in the early 1980s, Mary Gates, Bill's mother, headed up the executive committee of an NGO called the United Way of America.[19] The chairman of the International Business Machines Corporation (IBM), John Opel, sat on the same executive committee. Mrs Gates discussed her son's small software start-up, Microsoft, with Mr Opel, who then referred Bill and his company to other IBM executives. This referral led to IBM taking a chance on Microsoft as the developer of the MS-DOS (Microsoft Disk Operating System) for its first personal computer. In the wake of this collaboration, Microsoft rapidly went on to becomethe world's largest software company, and the rest, as they say, is history.

There is no doubt that the young Bill Gates was a very dedicated, talented and smart person, who at the time had expert skills that were scarce, with deep competency in a field that was about to revolutionize the world. But what would have become of him and the fledgling Microsoft had his mother not leveraged her network to help get her son the IBM deal? We will never know for sure, but what we do know is that the IBM deal served as the launching pad for Microsoft's meteoric rise to one of the biggest and most ubiquitous companies the world has ever seen.

THE THREE CORE FUNCTIONS OF A NETWORK

Microsoft and Bill Gates are not unique in having benefited from a network. Such stories are woven into the fabric of every successful company, but they are rarely publicized. Instead, founders and owners opt to tell the public exciting and awe-inspiring stories about their own hard work and perseverance, and their relentless pursuit of excellence. These factors are no doubt contributors to their success, but I can assure you the networks that they were plugged into played no lesser role.

Such networks can be instrumental in providing access to influential people who can:
- Create opportunities to help founders and their companies to scale quickly
- Offer exclusive insights and firsthand expertise
- Provide access to capital

These are essentially the three core functions that any network should serve. Let's take a closer look at them now.

CREATING
OPPORTUNITIES

I'm going to break down the opportunities that a network can create into three types: endorsement, commercial and access to other influential people.

One of the most powerful and effective forms of marketing is word of mouth. This holds true when it comes to the referrals or recommendations that people provide about you too. You can have the best resume and a long list of achievements, but if someone credible doesn't vouch for you by giving a genuine endorsement of who you are and what you've accomplished, it becomes hard for another person (perhaps someone considering you for a new job or a promotion) to validate your story. In fact, an endorsement from the right person can sometimes even result in securing you a position ahead of someone who has better credentials on paper.

Endorsements also create commercial opportunities. This is exemplified in the Microsoft story where John Opel opened the door for Microsoft to IBM. You can be introduced to people who want to do business with you, which provides you with a platform to engage with people who are, at the very least, curious about and interested in your product or service. Again, if the person who is making the referral is powerful and well respected, it makes it all the more likely that the person you are selling to will consider your product favourably because they themselves will probably want to create a positive impression on the person making the referral, for obvious reasons.

The right network will also create opportunities to access other value-creating networks, which has a multiplier effect. Networks have an exponential effect, especially when they are made up of diverse people – people who are from different places and have varying backgrounds. You want to connect with people who can connect you with other people, not people who will connect you to the same people you know. The latter is a closed network. Unless you already enjoy access to some real heavyweights who can create significant opportunities for you, a closed network is often a dead end. If, however, you connect with people from different backgrounds, outside of your circle of friends, family and colleagues, you create an open network that has a multiplier effect. This increases your impact, reach and ability to connect with others. These are leverage points for your skills and abilities, and they can be the deciding factor in your meteoric rise or unfortunate story of unrealized success.

PROVIDING ACCESS TO KNOWLEDGE AND SKILLS

It's becoming easier to access knowledge and learn new skills. The internet has democratized information and provided almost everyone with access to a great deal of knowledge that used to be difficult to get hold of. This has levelled the playing field somewhat. Unless you are willing to pay more than the average person can afford to access premium content, the chance of you gaining a skills and knowledge advantage is unlikely – that is, unless you can connect with people who can provide you with access to their own trademark knowledge and expertise born out of their own experience. This is the second function that a network should serve: access to unique knowledge and expertise that can help you to do whatever you are doing, better.

Early on in my career, I wasted countless hours trying to solve problems or get a unique perspective on a topic through my own independent research. Looking back, I realize that much of this time could have been saved had I been able to tap into the wisdom of subject matter experts or individuals with deep experience in the field. I know better now, which is why I know someone, or know someone who knows someone, who can provide me with solid insights and credible perspectives on several topics. In my consulting days at Deloitte, before kicking off a new engagement I would spend some time scouring the Deloitte global network for an expert in the industry relevant to the project or for someone who had completed a similar engagement. I would then connect with that person and spend 30 minutes to an hour getting insights from their experience before actually doing any other research or analysis. I found this to be hugely helpful in providing me with unique experiential knowledge of the subject matter of the engagement, which helped me to add more value to both my work and clients.

Beyond the specific knowledge and skills that some people can provide, I have found that through connecting with people, my capacity to think and process information has improved over time, too. The lens through which we see the world is the product of our social and environmental conditioning. This basically means that the networks we are exposed to have a profound impact on the way we perceive the world – and, consequently, our ability to make decisions and act in way that creates value in our professional and personal lives. By exposing yourself to others' unique perspectives and insights, you will expand your capacity to see things differently. This will not only broaden your horizons but also shape the way you think and see the world. However, I must highlight that this process is a mixed bag – you'll encounter both valuable insights and less helpful ones. So, exercise some discretion in choosing your network connections. Focus your time on those who share your values and aspirations. This is not to say that you should restrict yourself to people who are similar to you or likeminded. On the contrary, as pointed out above, you should aim to have a diverse network of people with different personal and professional backgrounds so that the perspectives and insights you are exposed to are varied too. Just make sure they are aligned to the path you are pursuing and things you want out of life and your career.

PROVIDING ACCESS TO CAPITAL

With the proliferation of technological advancement, especially over the past decade, the start-up space has been expanding at a rapid rate. Stories of incredible founders and their start-ups making a significant impact in their respective industries are all too common. The story usually breaks when venture funding comes through in one of the early rounds, either seed or now even pre-seed. But, before then, you rarely hear about these businesses or their founders. So the question is: How do they raise the capital to get their ideas off the ground? The answer is through their network.

To raise capital at the seed or even pre-seed stage, you need to demonstrate a 'proof of concept' for your product. Now, depending on the type of business you are trying to build, this can often require a decent amount of money as an investment to get things off the ground. You can have the best product or the most game-changing service in the world, but if you do not have the requisite capital, it's very unlikely that you will be able to do much. If you don't have a significant portfolio of assets, it's almost impossible to get a loan from a bank (nor would you want to get one with the extortionate interest rates that most personal loans carry). This is where your networks play a very powerful role. If you have a network of people who know you and trust your abilities, you can leverage this network to bootstrap and get your start-up off the ground. Sure, you may have to part with some equity to justify their investment, but the truth of the matter is you would never be able to do anything if you didn't have the capital anyway – 20% of something is always better than 100% of nothing.

Now that we have articulated what a network is and why it is important, lets discuss how to build one.

THREE PRINCIPLES FOR BUILDING A NETWORK

Before we get stuck into a plan to build a network, I want to provide you with some principles for networking up front. These are formulated out of my own experience over many years of contending with the joys and frustrations of engaging with people, which have culminated in an expanding network that has had a significant impact on my professional life.

1.
FOCUS ON QUALITY, NOT QUANTITY

You are going to encounter all kinds of weird and wonderful people along your journey. While it's important to increase the size of your network by connecting with people from different cultures and backgrounds, you must ensure that you invest most of your time building relationships with people who are aligned to your core values and to your mission, for the most part. Time is the most valuable resource and you should invest it where you get the best return. Building valuable relationships takes time and requires dedicated effort, often over many years. Trying to build relationships with people who have different value systems is frustrating, unsustainable and simply not worth the time and effort. They are distracting and the clash will inevitably lead to discord. You are much better off with a network of a few people where you invest time and effort in cultivating meaningful, value-adding relationships, rather than a series of superficial dalliances.

2.
ALL THAT GLITTERS IS NOT GUCCI

One the biggest lessons I've learned when it comes to people is that what you see is not always what you get. Appearances can be deceiving and people who make an extra effort to exude power and influence – usually in the way they speak, dress and behave – often lack substance and status. Many of them don't have the ability to create opportunities for others, though they may say, and even believe, that they can. Identifying such individuals isn't always straightforward, especially when you're just starting out. I'm not suggesting that you should entirely exclude those who fit this description from your network. Rather, I want to highlight the prevalence of this archetype both online (on professional networking sites) and perhaps within your workplace. This awareness can save you from investing time in relationships that end up going nowhere, allowing you to allocate more of your energy towards connecting with truly influential people. These are the individuals who have the ability and willingness to create meaningful opportunities for others.

3.
BE YOURSELF, SO YOU WILL NEVER HAVE TO SELL YOURSELF

The corporate world can appear intimidating from the outside. It looks like a place made up of sophisticated and intelligent people who conduct themselves perfectly, all the time. Let me assure you that this is not the case – far from it! So, don't give in to any misconception that you need to say and do things perfectly to succeed, or that you have to project an idealized version of yourself all the time. This will eventually lead to a disconnect from your authentic self (which, like everyone else includes quirks and flaws!) and this may in turn run counter to your attempts to create a good impression. My experience has taught me that those who you should be aiming to build relationships with are able to see beyond the false perceptions that people create. They are usually able to spot substance in a person and will likely be aware of the value you possess and the results you have produced, so you don't have to sell yourself to them. All you need to do is to be yourself and express yourself as authentically as you possibly can. There is no need to replicate the superficial model of corporate success that many are desperately trying to play out. Embracing your true self will make you stand out, and over time, you'll naturally attract the kind of folks who'll be a real asset to your network.

HOW TO BUILD
A NETWORK

Now that we've laid out some basic principles, let's outline an action plan to build a professional network.

1.
START WITH
WHO YOU KNOW

Begin by compiling a list of people that you know or have encountered – friends, family, colleagues, acquaintances from seminars, workshops or conferences. Then list their job title and their profession or the industry they work in and start grouping them accordingly. Identify the people you know the best within the industry and profession groups that are relevant to you, and start reaching out to them on whatever medium you feel comfortable with. Personally, I'm a bit old-school when it comes to engaging with people and my preference is face-to-face conversation. So, I start with a call or a message to set up some time to chat in-person. I prepare for the meeting by developing a structure and listing the points that I want to discuss. This ensures that I get what I need out of the conversation and demonstrates my respect for the other person's time, which bodes well for future meetings.

Sometimes the script completely falls away – be open to that happening too. You may go into the conversation wanting a make a good impression by asking clear, well-considered questions, only to find that the other person wants to know more about you and wants to talk less about themselves. This is the beauty of conversation and human connection, and it is where a lot of the magic happens, so don't try to adjust the course. Go with it, be yourself and trust that the conversation will land in a good place.

Starting with the people you know gives you a good opportunity to build some confidence, learn some professional conversational skills and get some experience at networking within a safe environment. And, if those familiar people happen to wield influence in their respective fields and influence, all the better.

2.
ATTEND EVENTS

Take the time and make the investment (where the cost is justified) to attend conferences and similar types of events. These occasions offer fertile ground for forging connections, given that attendees generally have a shared purpose for being there. The key is not to spend too much time with one person. You want to maximize your opportunities to meet as many people as possible to increase your chances of connecting with influential people. The trick you need to master in such situations is to make yourself as memorable as possible – in a good way, of course. Running naked through the event might get you noticed, but not in the way you want! The goal is to create a brief yet memorable interaction that extends beyond the event itself. One way to do this is to do some research into the industry or field related to the event. Try and remember some interesting or noteworthy developments that people may be interested in (no need to regurgitate data like a parrot – nobody's a fan of that). Study the numbers and facts, and form your own insights and opinions. This is far more effective and leads to meaningful conversation. Be sure to collect business cards or contact details, and spend some time debriefing after the event by sifting out the people with whom you would like to continue engaging. Then, send an email to them to keep the conversation going and to stay on their radar.

Now, you might be thinking, "But I'm an introvert and I hate being forced to connect with people I don't know." Don't worry, I totally get it – I was in the same boat. My advice? Start small. Aim to strike a conversation with just one person. Often, they might even initiate contact first. These interactions gradually build confidence, making it easier to repeat the process.

Finally, remember that it's not just meeting new people on the outside that matters. It is absolutely critical for you to connect with people inside your organization too. These internal relationships can foster workplace collaboration, provide new insights and create a supportive environment that enhances your professional journey.

Remember, a robust network consists of people both within and outside your workplace and can be a powerful driver in achieving your career goals.

3.
CONNECT WITH
PEOPLE ONLINE

As I write this, LinkedIn is probably the best place to connect with professional people online. I have found it to be an immensely powerful networking tool that has helped me to connect with people across the globe, simply by sending them an introductory message. Of course, I have not received replies to many of my requests, but I have managed to secure some time with people who add value to my network for different reasons. I'm certainly not proposing that you go on a random messaging spree, but rather a thoughtful approach aimed at connecting with those who bring value to your network – experts in your field, industry leaders or potential colleagues.

To make the most of LinkedIn, ensure that your profile is up to date and that it is showcasing you and your professional story in the best possible way. Send a concise, professional message highlighting the reason for your message and clearly articulating what you hope to get out of connecting with the person. You have nothing to lose.

While the traditional office environment remains a part of our work landscape, the adoption of remote and more flexible 'hybrid' work arrangements has steadily been on the rise. As such, you may find that senior, influential people at your organization who were previously almost impossible to reach and secure time with are now much more accessible.

4.
GET INVOLVED IN SHARED ACTIVITIES

Get involved in shared activities such as charitable initiatives, group sports, profession-based meet-up groups and community services. Be selective about those that you choose. You must have both a genuine interest in the activity and a commitment to stick to any required programme. Also, try to get a sense of the type of people that you will be interacting with. Again, if these people are not aligned with your value system or are not the types you want in your network, it may be a fruitless effort and a waste of valuable time.

If you're able to identify a shared activity that you have competency or an interest in and there are people participating that you want to connect with, you've struck gold! The force of shared purpose is very powerful when it comes to connecting with people and it can lead to some great opportunities, as was the case for Microsoft. Bill Gates's mother and the chairman of IBM had a shared purpose by sitting on the board of the NGO.

BUILDING RELATIONSHIPS

The most important thing to remember when it comes to building a network is that you are connecting with people – fellow humans who are governed by complex mental and emotional algorithms. The objective is ultimately to make a positive impression on people and get them to think and feel good things so that they connect with you. This is an expansive topic and could probably appear on a list of the most-written-about areas in business; nevertheless, in a chapter on building a network, it is essential to dedicate a few paragraphs to the process of building relationships. The following are tips and insights that have served me well over my career, and continue to do so.

1.
BE AN EMPATHETIC LISTENER

I have found listening to be one of the most powerful means to connect with people – I'm talking about active listening and not just hearing what the other person is saying. This requires the listener to be as present as they possibly can and to listen without feeling the need to respond. Suspend your judgements and leave your biases at the door. Be open and prepared to be exposed to thoughts, ideas and concepts that may challenge you and your belief system. You don't have to accept them or agree with them. The point is to listen and have empathy – seeing the world in the same way another person sees it. When you listen deeply, you naturally become empathetic. This has an incredibly powerful effect on the other person and your ability to connect with them – it is where the magic starts to happen.

2.
PAY ATTENTION TO THE SMALL DETAILS

Our profession is just one aspect of our lives – there is a whole other life that often is more important to people. It is kept out of public view for the most part, but sometimes people talk about their families and other things that are important to them. If you want to be memorable and make an impact on a person, remember the small details like the names of their kids or their dog, their favourite hobby, or where they are planning to go over the holidays. When you meet them again, weave those details into the conversation. It demonstrates to them that you care enough to remember and it has a profound effect.

Another small but important detail is knowing people's names and using those names when speaking to them. I will never forget the day David Williams joined my then employer, Maersk, as Managing Director for Southern Africa. I was a clerk at the time (the analyst equivalent of today), so literally right at the bottom of the ladder. David was in charge of a huge business that employed a few thousand people at least. But when he walked through the office he made a point of greeting each and every one of us with a smile and by name. I looked at him in awe and remember feeling super-motivated, thinking, "This guy actually knows my name!" For the duration of my time at Maersk, whenever I saw David he would greet me with his trademark smile and use my name. This had a profound effect on me. I felt recognized and this served to motivate me in a very significant way.

Since then I have always made a point of learning people's names. I have found that simply addressing them by their name in a conversation seems to jolt their attention towards me and it becomes clear that they suddenly feel good about themselves for a moment. It can be difficult to learn and remember people's names, but make a point of putting in the effort to do so and then use a person's name in your conversation every so often. This simple networking hack has a remarkable effect when it comes to connecting with people.

3.
DON'T CRITICIZE

This one is a lot harder to get right. We all need criticism, but very few take it without offence, and offending a person is a certain way to harm your relationship with them. So if someone says something that you believe to be factually incorrect, especially when other people are around, at all costs avoid the urge to display your own superior knowledge by correcting the person directly. I am not suggesting that you allow ignorance to prevail. Rather I am suggesting, firstly, that you approach the correction within a setting that is private and, secondly, that you do so in such a way that the person does not feel attacked or offended (i.e. as gently as possible). Maybe even consider whether the point is worth correcting in the first place. If there are no moral or ethical implications or the potential for a significant negative impact, let it slide. The cost of correcting a person, whether in public or private, is often far greater than the cost of allowing some wrong statistic to prevail. Read the room, and learn to know what is worth correcting and what is not.

On the flip side, you need to learn how to let people know that they have done something or said something to offend you. Perhaps the most critical consideration here is not to react from a place of anger or strong emotion – obvious enough, but much harder to do when someone has upset you. Build the emotional resilience you need to gracefully manage your emotions in conflict situations, and when addressing the matter with the other person, don't attack. Discuss, engage and explore with the mindset of actually resolving the issue and getting your point across rather than inflicting pain or shame on people. Your ability to handle such situations gracefully can speak volumes and carry you far.

4.
MAKE PEOPLE FEEL GOOD ABOUT THEMSELVES

Think about the last time someone paid you a compliment or said something really nice about you. If you're not a nihilistic masochist, you probably felt really good about yourself. You likely felt energized and inspired, and you now likely associate positive thoughts and feelings with the person and are inclined towards engaging with them in the future. Compliment the work of others and the impact that they are making. It costs you absolutely nothing. Stretch the truth if you have to – but be tactful! The point is to convey positive words to create positive emotions, which lies at the heart of connecting with people. Master this, and you will be arming yourself with a powerful tool for building a network of valuable relationships that will fuel your growth, both personally and professionally. In words that have been attributed to various authors, including the late, great American poet Maya Angelou, "People will forget what you said and what you did, but they will never forget how you made them feel."

A FINAL NOTE ON NETWORKING

I would argue that a significant portion of your corporate success is a function of your ability to network and connect with people. You can be the smartest, most hard-working person in the organization, but if you are not able to connect and work well with people, it's unlikely that you will succeed at the highest levels. You need to build a network of supporters and promoters around you – people who are willing to stick their necks out for you and vouch for your abilities. Naturally, being able to form relationships with these people is a critical part of them becoming advocates for you and willing to create opportunities for you to thrive. There's a saying that states, 'your network is your net worth.' I'm a firm believer in this. Now go out there and build an army!

CHAPTER 6

LEARN HOW TO HANDLE DIFFICULT PEOPLE

BY MATT

One thing that is certain to happen in the corporate world is that you will encounter a good variety of people. Sadly, some of these people just won't be very nice at all. This will not just happen once – it will happen a few times, and the only way to survive these experiences (some of which may last years) is to have a very specific mindset and plan. As time goes on, your strategy will evolve. For example, in your earlier years you might need to be careful about 'taking people on' – there are some battles you may just want to leave for the time being (of course, any boundary crossing or anything ethically problematic shouldn't ever be brushed aside). But as you get more senior, and build a stronger reputation, there will be instances where you can stand up to these people directly, provided you are thoughtful about how you do it.

There is no single definition of a 'difficult person.' You might describe these people with words that I won't venture to set down here. Fundamentally, there is a significant level of subjectivity in definitions of this type of person, because they are based on highly personal experiences. To be clear, just because someone is stern or disagrees with you does not mean they are the type of person I am talking about here. With that said, let me try to be a little more specific. This type of person is likely to have some (or all) of the following traits:

- **Their beliefs:** In most instances, they think about their own welfare before the welfare of others.
- **Their actions:** Either directly or indirectly, they try to make other people look bad while making themselves look good.
- **The root cause:** Unbeknownst to their colleagues, they will usually have had some bad experience(s)

in the past that drives this behaviour (e.g. being looked over for a promotion, being bullied when they were younger). While this doesn't justify difficult behaviour, recognizing this serves as a reminder that they too are human and shaped by their own history.

But these traits just scratch the surface because they are very broad. Difficult people can be divided into three major types (there are likely more, but these are arguably the main ones):

- **The narcissist:** This person may suck you in and spit you out. The dictionary defines a narcissist as some who is "extremely self-centered with an exaggerated sense of self-importance" and notes that the word 'narcissistic' means "marked by or characteristic of excessive admiration of or infatuation with oneself."[20]
- **The chaotic colleague:** This is someone who is just all over the place but expects you to drop everything you're doing when they decide they need something from you (with no warning).
- **The micro-manager:** This person will probably leave you with emotional scars. They sit over your shoulder watching your every move. In no time at all, you'll know what perfume or cologne they use because they will be very close, always! In a remote work setting they might be pinging you every 30 minutes to see how things are going.

WHY DO WE ALWAYS SEEM TO HAVE THESE PEOPLE IN ORGANIZATIONS?

The simplest answer to this question is that the world is full of weird and wonderful people. So, if there is a distribution of 'person types' in an organization, you have to expect to come across many different types – and, yes, this includes the difficult ones too.

As time goes on, however, you'll come to realize that this group must be overrepresented. You might start wondering how is it that every team or organization you join has one (or many) – surely this can't be right? Are you just unlucky? Should you keep changing roles until you find a team that doesn't have one?

No! There are two reasons it seems like you are always coming across these people. Firstly, they tend to do well in corporate settings, very often as managers (although not leaders – true leadership usually requires the very opposites of the three traits listed above). Managing people is a very tough thing to get right. Good managers who are also emerging leaders will try to strike a balance between achieving short-term business outcomes and focusing on medium- and longer-term factors that relate to the personal development and employee experience of their team members. The difficulty is that sometimes the 'big boss' doesn't want managers making this trade-off themselves (it can be risky), and in these instances they are likely to have a bias (assuming they are risk averse) towards the types of people who prioritize short-term business objectives above all else. In short, sometimes, in the eyes of an anxious executive team, mean and nasty people make for good managers because they have no problem ordering people around.

The second reason it seems like you are always coming across these people is that their personality style and impact on you will *feel* greater than their actual presence. Let's imagine you work in a division of 50 people and over the years you've come to identify two or three of these nasty types. Even though they make up only 4–6% of the team, it will often *feel* as though they are everywhere. There are probably two reasons for this. Firstly, they likely talk more often, and over other team members. So, in team meetings, their 'share of voice' is significantly larger than their actual representation. But secondly – and this is probably the real driver – the *types* of things they say to you or to the team in group settings do not live and die in meetings. They are often things that sit in your mind for hours (or days) after the session. The combination of the type of things they say and the way people's minds tend to work (over-analysing these interactions) results in a significant magnification effect.[21]

HOW SHOULD YOU HANDLE THIS TYPE OF PERSON?

Most likely these people will make you very angry in some instances and deeply upset in others. I have found the insights from executive coach Michele Woodward, workplace bullying expert Gary Namie (as reported by Amy Gallo), and Stanford University psychologist Robert J. Sutton to be useful in helping me to form a coherent perspective on this question.[22]

I'm going to break down the advice into three main steps:

1. Take a step back and carefully consider what is driving the person's behaviour while remaining professional yourself
2. Take practical short-term steps to help yourself: be direct and leverage your network to assist you
3. If things don't improve, get real: demonstrate the business cost but know the limits

Let's consider each of these in turn. But first, a point of clarification: the steps here relate to the kinds of interpersonal difficulties that can happen between any two people. If you are facing something more targeted, such as racial or gender-based discrimination, it should be dealt with in a more formal manner from the start, such as by taking your concerns to HR. We are well into the 21st century – gone are the days when you needed to 'suck it up' in such cases. Today, standing up for yourself and your rights makes you a better (emerging) leader.

1.
TAKE A STEP BACK

Understand what is driving the person's behaviour
If I think about my own experiences, most of the time I've dealt with really awful people there were very simple and clear underlying factors. Let me give you an example. The interaction was with a client rather than an colleague, but the dynamics of the situation could just as easily apply to an internal situation.

I was running a small project in the Cape region of South Africa and one of my team's clients was being a pain. In this instance I was trying to update a set of agreements between an acquiring company and the acquiree. The difficult person was in the acquiree organization, and I needed to interact with them daily. It didn't help that I was a twenty-something with a bad haircut and this was an experienced commercial contract expert. But it was more than that – I felt as though he hated me before I said a word. I realized, though, that he didn't hate me. He hated that his team was being bought and he really didn't like hearing any views (other than his own) about commercial arrangements.

To deal with this kind of situation you need to start by understanding what drives the person's behaviour. The researchers I mentioned above suggest that the reason people start to 'act out' is because their ego feels threatened by you or the work you are doing. This can result in really bad behaviour even from accomplished and respected senior leaders in business. You would be surprised to see how fragile egos can be. If you are smart, hard-working and well-liked by your peers, guess what? You're very likely to be disliked by someone slightly senior to you because you're a threat. In some cases you therefore need to take the extra time to show your boss gratitude – show them you respect them and that you'd like to learn. This can go a long way in smoothing things over.

Stay professional: Double check your behaviour

In these situations you also need to perform some self-reflection and some moderation. Think back and reflect on the interactions you've had with this person. Ask the tough question of yourself – what have you done that's contributed to the problem?

Self-reflection requires introspection. To what extent are you behaving in a certain way? If your organization's culture is competitive and impolite, have you been absorbed by these norms and has this changed the way you interact with the team? Aside from your behaviour, check that you haven't misunderstood what someone else is doing or saying. Often people have different backgrounds, expectations and working styles, and you will need to keep this in mind. This is not to say you should just back down. Rather, it emphasizes the importance of pausing to take a moment and check yourself.

After engaging in this introspection, make sure you keep things professional going forward. At times you'll experience a strong desire to lash out. This might feel good in the short term, but it'll reduce your credibility down the line.

2.
TAKE PRACTICAL
SHORT-TERM STEPS
TO HELP YOURSELF

Be direct: Stand up for yourself

Provided you are certain that your actions will always remain professional, it may be useful (at the right time) to directly call out someone's bad behaviour. This is likely to be very difficult the first time you do it. But, if done correctly, it may have a massive impact on how the individual interacts with you in the future.

I'll quickly share another story. A few years back when I started a new job, I found that one of the team members and I didn't get along very well. This particular person would often send very short and quite aggressive emails to me. At first I ignored the aggressiveness and tried to stay positive, but I must admit that after some time it started to wear me down. I honestly don't know how I built up the courage, but this person and I had a one-on-one call about another topic (something like a review of a financial model). At the beginning of the call I paused and said, "Before we start, do you mind if we quickly discuss something unrelated?" When I got the "Yes," my heart started to beat very quickly. I almost lost my breath. I don't remember exactly what I said but it was something like this: "Do you remember that email you sent me? Well... I found the tone to be a little unprofessional and I didn't like that... I just wanted to let you know how I felt about it." Done. Those few short sentences were so hard to get out, but I felt relieved and happy that I'd managed it. The reaction was initially silence, and then the person said, "Okay... I didn't realize that." I replied, "No problem – like I said I just wanted you to know how it came across to me... Let's move on and discuss the financial model."

Was the meeting a little awkward – for sure! Did I survive? Without doubt. Did I receive another nasty mail? No.

Get help: Leverage your network
Another option you have, especially if you try the method above and it doesn't work, is to leverage your network in the office. Provided you are not brand new in the role, you will have connected, and even made friends, with some of your colleagues. They might include peers as well as team members who are senior to you. Let's call this your 'crew.' This is a great situation where you can use your crew to help.

Amy Gallo has advice on what to do, again quoting Michele Woodward:

> "Everybody should have alliances at work – peers and people above and below, who can be your advocates and champions," says Woodward. Talk to those supporters and see what they can do to help, whether it's simply confirming your

perspective or speaking on your behalf. Of course, you may need to escalate the situation to someone more senior or to HR. But before that, "you owe it to the relationship to try to solve it informally," says Woodward.[23]

3.
IF THINGS DON'T IMPROVE, TAKE FURTHER ACTION

Demonstrate the business cost

If you've gone through the steps above with no effect, you may need to take formal action. Assuming your direct boss isn't the aggressor, let them know that you would like to raise an issue. Typically, you should let someone in your chain of command know, as well as going directly to HR to explain the situation. Be open and honest about what has gone on and suggest ways you think the situation can be resolved (if it can be). Do your best to stay professional and focus on explaining how the actions of this person are not only impacting you but also the business more broadly. As much as organizations don't like to admit it, if you are able to show a negative business impact, things might move a lot more quickly.

Know the limits

There are also times when even taking some of the formal steps above won't deliver the right outcome. I think this is especially true in some emerging markets and it is certainly the case in South Africa. I continue to believe that many leaders are not on top of topics relating to diversity and inclusion. This isn't something you should have to suffer through, especially if you've made an effort to offer solutions. So, if you have tried everything above and things just haven't changed, you may need to contemplate seeking a more supportive and progressive company – a decision that might entail leaving.

This is tough advice, because it may feel wrong to walk away and leave a tough situation, but I think that employees should increasingly be activist when it comes to these matters. Most corporates have not yet faced the music, and what I hope is that strong-willed and talented employees will move to organizations that match their values, and away from those that don't. In the medium term, those organizations that can't change with the times will lose the war for talent and will quickly lose their ability to compete in the market.

WHAT IF *YOU* ARE A DIFFICULT PERSON (OF THE GENERAL TYPE)?

This is where it gets real! Check yourself – ask for feedback, and just accept that you may need to make some changes. Let me be honest, I like to think that I'm 'not difficult' the vast majority of the time, but I'm sure there are times I've created minor frustrations.

Some people would argue that there are times when it's okay to be painful, such as during high-pressure, short-term projects. However, more broadly, being a difficult person leads to low team morale and can have a negative impact on the business. If you're struggling with this in yourself, you'll probably need to start by admitting you have a problem – for example, if you're mean or unreasonable, perhaps it's because you have a fragile ego. Accept it, get over it and ask the people around you for advice. This is easier said than done, but if you have a genuine interest in improving, the people around you will appreciate it massively.

This is especially important if, after a few years of work, you're trusted to lead a small team. This stuff is important. It matters for you but it matters more for other people – never forget that.

Here are a few ways you can improve your team.

1.
CREATE AN ENVIRONMENT
OF INCLUSION AND
SELF-AWARENESS

First up, create an inclusive environment. It is critical to create a culture of belonging and care that ensures you have a positive work environment in which everyone is included and feels respected. This is easier said than done, but it is certainly worth the effort. Most evidence suggests that this will create happier and harder-working team members who are focused on the success of the group rather than their own success as individuals.[24] What this means for you is setting the right behavioural norms. Treat everyone with the respect and dignity they deserve, push yourself to listen to new ideas that challenge your own, and create spaces for you and your team to reflect on the ways you work together.

It is key to identify those team members who can help this initiative, as Sanyin Siang – CEO coach, adviser to Google Ventures and the executive director of Duke University's Coach K Center on Leadership and Ethics – points out:

> Recognize the value of team members who have a natural talent for fostering inter- and intra-team relationships. In the Industrial Age model of productivity, the deep value of such superpowers

often went unrecognized. But these teammates can be the emotional glue for a team, cross-pollinators of valuable information or increase the 'joy capital' of work for everyone.[25]

When team members excel in this space, ensure they are recognized for their work. Show gratitude for the contributions they are making. Your team members want to be noticed when they try hard and get it right – do not ever forget to make that a priority. This creates a virtuous cycle of motivation, production, feedback and value creation.

Author Skye Schooley makes this point well:

Ask your team what types of recognition they prefer and how often they would like team events to occur. These occasions can be related to work, volunteering or just general fun, but take precautions to ensure that each event is inclusive and appropriate for your workplace.[26]

Sudhanshu Palsule makes the point that something that significantly supports inclusion is the practice of self-awareness. The best managers are learning and growing alongside their team and creating the space for growth to be possible. This fundamentally requires you to have created an environment of psychological safety. Palsule focuses on 21st-century leadership and brings together the latest research emerging from neurology and cognitive psychology:

One of the biggest and the most primeval of all human needs is the need to belong. This need was probably sculpted into the human brain in the plains of the African savannah a hundred thousand years ago. Belonging not only provides security, it engenders feelings of commitment and following. During a crisis, the need to belong is amplified several times over.

There is no one way of engendering the feeling of belonging and safety. It can take many forms including regularly checking in with others; showing appreciation for their work; helping them connect with the larger purpose of the work they do; allowing for mistakes, etc. The term 'psychological safety' was first used in 1990 by William Kahn who described it as "being able to show and employ one's self without fear of negative consequences to self-image, status or career." Anxiety in the current context is natural and needs expression. However, in many organizations, there is the pressure – either self-inflicted or through peer actions – to cover up the anxiety. Gender often plays a role here and there is a fear many men have of coming across as weak and ineffective if they are to talk about their anxieties. Creating psychological safety is therefore also about helping the others express and share their anxiety knowing that they are not being judged. A problem shared is a problem halved is not just an old saying, it is based on scientific evidence.[27]

You therefore need to ensure that you are encouraging all team members (including yourself) to be self-aware in the spirit of psychological safety. Your facial expressions, body language, words and actions all contribute to this environment and it is up to you to get this right. You need to be aware of the impact you are having – both the intentional and the unintentional. Again, one of the best ways to encourage this mindset and behaviour in your own work and throughout your team is to foster learning. If you and everyone else are learning something new each week or each month, there is no space for intolerance because everyone is grappling with change together.

2.
KNOW YOUR TEAM AND LEARN HOW TO WORK WITH THEM

Unless your team is made up of a collection of robots (not so much of a joke as it might have been a few years ago, but still not an imminent prospect), you'll need to connect with people and get to know them. I'm not suggesting that you have to like and be friends with everyone on your team, but you do need to show genuine interest and understand the things that motivate people – the things they like and don't like. This matters for how you construct roles and responsibilities. Keep in mind that everyone will have different strengths and development areas, and understanding the characteristics behind these will enable you to create a positive working environment.

You can get to know your team in many ways. Of course, you can observe people, but don't stare too much – they might think you're creepy. Build formal and informal occasions where everyone can get to know each other better. Make sure these are fun and purposeful, and you can be assured the group dynamics will solidify. But on top of this you can simply just take the time to ask people questions. A *Harvard Business Review* article suggests asking a question such as "What was the best day you've had at work in the last three months?" to get individuals thinking about the work and experiences that keep them motivated.[28] (On a side note, if the answer is that the best day they had at work was the company off-site where no work was done, then you might have another challenge on your hands.) It's probably also prudent to ask for examples of experiences that left team members feeling demotivated or frustrated.

Getting to know your team is also an important step in moving up the ladder – not just as a manager but as a leader. There's a pretty big stack of academic literature on leadership, some of which is better than the rest. Let me summarize it as follows: unless you are in a very particular setting, the old conception of the 'heroic' leader who runs the show, leads 'from the front,' and was 'born to lead' is pretty much dead. You should be reading this and celebrating – that approach led to some pretty bad behaviour and some even worse outcomes.

What's replaced this conception is harder to explain. It's not the opposite – a soft, cuddly teddy-bear leader giving out free hugs all day. Instead, modern leaders are required to perform a difficult (and ever changing) balancing act. You will need to continue to guide and steer your team, but you will have to do so in a way that creates joint accountability and a real sense of togetherness.

Skye Schooley quotes executive coach Ora Shtull, who says:

> If you don't break the addiction to doing it all, you won't have the capacity to step up and do more senior stuff. ... Letting go involves delegating. But it's important to note that delegating doesn't mean deserting the team or sacrificing accountability.[29]

I quite like the way Schooley herself says:

> As a manager, you have a different set of responsibilities from your entry-level team members, but you should still get your hands dirty. Additionally, you should include your team in decision-making processes. According to Kimble's Boss Barometer Report, 74% of American workers surveyed said they prefer a collaborative working culture to one where the boss makes most of the decisions.[30]

3.
COMMUNICATE GOALS
AND PLAY THE COACH

The last thing to consider here – and probably the puzzle piece that will lead to the best relationship-building – is communication and coaching. Communication is the foundation of good working relationships, and it enables you and your team to be aligned on your goals. A lot has been written about goal-setting. One of the simplest ways to test whether the goals you are setting make sense comes from the SMART framework: make sure your goals are specific, measurable, achievable, realistic and time bound.[31] Importantly, every team member should be contributing to the creation and interpretation of goals. This ensures that high-level organizational goals are translated into team and individual goals and that those lower-level goals encourage behaviour that aligns with the highest-level objectives.

Of course, this cannot be a one-off exercise. Goals are not set and left. Goals are set to be reviewed – constantly. This creates an expectation that goals set should be goals met. The entire team should review and track their progress against their goals in a structured manner. This can be done through a series of goal check-ins. These conversations may be tough at times, because it is very often difficult to actually achieve complex goals, but the point for you as a leader is to listen and learn. These should always be two-way conversations.

As Skye Schooley points out, "Great leaders don't just listen; they listen to understand." She quotes Xan Raskin, founder and CEO of Artixan Consulting Group LLC, who says: "Making sure your employees know you not only heard them, but you understand – even if you disagree – goes a long way to building a long-term rapport with employees."[32]

The next level up from communication, especially around goals, is coaching team members through the journey – these processes go hand in hand. 'Coach' is a term that's bandied about a lot in corporate environments, so when I started writing this chapter I thought I'd see what the dictionaries have to say. The *Cambridge Dictionary* calls it: "someone whose job is to teach people to improve at a sport, skill, or school subject."[33] But a better definition for our purposes comes from *Merriam-Webster*: "to train intensively (as by instruction and demonstration)."[34] Keep that in mind: coaching is fundamentally about training – it is about setting up scenarios that adjust for risk and that allow team members to practise key skills.

I also quite like what some people have said to me – that a coach is someone "who has your back." A coach is therefore also someone who acts as an advocate for their team members. This makes for a difficult balancing act – you've got to hold the team to account but give them every opportunity to be the best version of themselves. Cheesy but true. This is likely to create a positive environment with solid motivation, and the highest chances of delivering high-quality work.

To quote Ora Shtull once again:

Effective managers coach by asking questions, empowering their team members to think deeply and generate solutions. ... In turn, team members gain confidence and grow, and ultimately become amazing bosses themselves.[35]

You should let employees know you care about their career progression. This means providing team members with the development they need to succeed in the working environment. Good managers (and coaches) are not threatened by the growth and success of their employees; instead, they embrace and encourage change. This is probably the most important – but the hardest – thing to get right, as it requires you to lose your ego!

CHAPTER 7

MAKE BETTER AND MORE ETHICAL BUSINESS DECISIONS

BY MATT

Writing a chapter on business ethics might seem like a simple task because there is so much literature and thought leadership available, but two things make it quite difficult. Firstly, because there is so much information already available, it's pretty darn difficult to sift through everything to determine the right approach. Secondly, it's also tricky to convert theories and ideas about ethics into something that is truly applicable and useful in everyday settings.

This chapter starts by making the case that we need to seriously review how we think about ethics in business settings. Then I'll share some reflections on ethical frameworks and which ones I've found most useful. Next, I'm going to share a couple of examples highlighting how these frameworks could be applied to make better decisions (here I'll be as practical as possible, sharing examples from my own career). Finally, to provide further context, I'll outline five major cases of fraud from around the world to examine how ethics might have led to better outcomes.

Let's first very quickly define business ethics for the purposes of this chapter. A definition in the *International Encyclopedia of Ethics* points out that while some elements of business ethics relate to "how individuals in the business world ought to behave," other elements relate to how individuals are "surrounded by layers of issues involving organizations and institutions."[36] So business ethics is not just about individuals – it is also about organizations and institutions more broadly.

THE CASE FOR ETHICS

Let's start with why this matters so much. Two simple points are relevant. Firstly, businesses and employees aren't getting it right at the moment. One thing the world is not short of is a good private (and public) sector scandal. We are all aware of the significant corruption problem faced in the public sector. But on top of this, and in some cases linked closely to it, we see multiple examples of unethical practice in the private sector too. The Steinhoff scandal is just one well-known example of corrupt practice in the private sector, but there are many more (as mentioned, the final section of this chapter explores five such cases in detail, including the Steinhoff scandal). It is certainly the case that the business leaders in the market have failed to deliver an ethical vision for their respective industries.

Secondly, because of many organizations' size and reach, when things go wrong, the impact can be significant. There are often far-reaching consequences for employees, families and communities. In many of these cases, large numbers of employees have lost their jobs, but the impact continues downstream to family members and communities.

PRINCIPLES

So how do we navigate such difficult territory? It's probably best to start by making an important distinction, and that is the distinction between the application of principles – say, through the law, regulation and professional bodies' policies – and the development of ethical principles themselves. The complexity we find ourselves in today relates (in part) to the fact that applied ethics is not sufficient to deal with all the complex ethical issues we face in our working lives. This means, I believe, that young people and emerging leaders need to be equipped with an understating of the laws, policies and regulations applicable in their environments, but also some more foundational (or theoretical) ethical principles that can help them to navigate complex territory.

If you want to read up on the law and organizational policies, I highly encourage you to do that, but we won't be covering those topics here. Rather, I'm going to leverage some simple theoretical principles to help you navigate some ethical dilemmas. As a side note, there is no single agreed-upon academic ethical theory – there are a few, each with their own nuances.

Very quickly, let's introduce a spectrum on which we can consider theories. On one end of the spectrum is a set of absolutist or universal theories. These theories spell out very specific and particular rules that (they claim) should apply in all settings. On the other end of the spectrum are theories embedded in relativism. In the extreme, these theories say that there are absolutely no rules or principles that can or should be applied but rather that ethics is entirely in the eye of the beholder. Each person or community can and should develop their own ethical norms (no matter what they are) and nobody should be able to tell them otherwise. The extreme ends of the spectrum are academically interesting but cannot offer us the answers we need in more complex real-world environments. Better theories are typically somewhere in the middle, and I'm going to focus on one useful example in the following paragraphs.

The theory I'm going to discuss was developed by John Rawls in his seminal work *A Theory of Justice*, published in 1971.[37] I've found two of Rawls's concepts to be very useful when thinking about tough ethical decisions. Firstly, there is the "veil of ignorance." This means that when we are deciding how to treat other people or organizations, we should try to imagine we have been (in Rawls's words) "born into their lives." This is, of course, the basic logic behind empathy, but the idea is to seriously consider how you would like to be treated – in other words, what you would consider fair if you occupied someone else's position in the lottery of life.

The second of Rawls's concepts that I find especially useful comes from a distinction between endowments and choices. Endowments are things we are all born with and that we didn't chose (e.g. race, sex, height and eye colour) whereas choices are, very obviously, things we have control over and where we get to determine an outcome (a simple example is how hard we work on something). While there are some sticky issues here (and I won't go down that rabbit hole), Rawls suggests that, as much as possible, people should face consequences (rewards or punishments) for things they choose, but should not face consequences for things they didn't choose (i.e. their endowments). This is the very simple foundation of why, to choose one possibility as an example, we might have a problem with racism and its consequences – because people don't choose their race.

APPLICATIONS

I have come across various ethical dilemmas during my career. Here are a couple of real-world examples and some thoughts on how they could have turned out better if a more ethical framework had been used.

CHILDCARE

In practice, it is really important to keep your finger on the ethical pulse. Here's a simple example that happened a few years back while I was working at a big firm. In this company, there was a set of project delivery teams doing specific work for the clients. The team I was in had about eight members, one of whom was a partner. Partners would have a dedicated assistant who would help significantly with the team's logistics.

In one particular situation, the team members were arranging a weekend getaway to celebrate the end of a project. The full team, including the assistant, were invited. The lowest paid delivery team member probably earned double the salary of the assistant – who, by the way, was a single mother. The full team RSVP'd positively, except the assistant, who couldn't stay away from home for the one night that was being spent out of town. As part of her reply, she explained that she couldn't find or afford a babysitter for the night.

I happened to be the person organizing the event. I asked the partner if we should cover an expense item for childcare to enable the assistant to join the team. The answer was no. This was bullshit!

Was this required by the law? No. Was this required by company policy? No. Was this decent and probably the thing we should have done? Yes, but it's only by referring to our ethical framework and stepping behind the "veil of ignorance" that we understand why.

MATERNITY AND PATERNITY LEAVE

A second example – a personal favourite of mine – relates to the archaic policies around maternity and paternity leave in many parts of the world. This is one I have debated at length with more senior team members in an organization.

What we are used to in many markets, including in South Africa, is a policy that goes something like this. Maternity leave might sit at around four months, while paternity leave might sit at one or two weeks. At first glance it might seem possible to rationalize this policy. Women, simply through their biology, bear a significant burden when it comes to childbirth. Surely, then, they should have extended paid leave while they recover and take care of the newborn baby. Men, on the other hand, don't really need the time off and can spend a week or two at home but should return to work soon afterwards.

So, what's the problem? There are lots of ways to describe why this very common practice is actually deeply problematic. For me the following scenario is the simplest way to encapsulate the issues. Imagine that a man and a woman start working at Company X at the same time. Now imagine they fall in love and decide to have a child together. If this common policy stands then what plays out is usually the following: the mother of the child takes four months away from work (as she should) to help with the very important early period of taking care of a newborn baby. The father takes two weeks to help out at home and returns to work after that.

This might appear, at first glance, to be beneficial to the mother, who gets more paid time away from work. But in actual fact there is something else going on. What the policy implies is that the company expects that a mother *should* bear the much more significant burden of childcare relative to the father. Women are then characterized by having greater duties at home relative to men. A fairer situation would be one in which both mother and father contribute equally at home – in policy terms, they should both be offered a full four months. So the first problem is simply related to fairness.

But the second problem is that this policy explicitly disadvantages women in the corporate space. If women all over the world are taking four months of maternity leave (or more) and men are only taking two weeks, then over time, and on average, women will have slower career trajectories. Taking around four months away from work is significant. In many cases, this can lead to the following consequences – relative to men:

- Women are less likely to be promoted as quickly as men
- Women are less likely to achieve bonus targets
- Women are less likely to achieve the same salary increases
- Women are perceived as less likely to be able to manage long, complex projects because they are more likely (on average) to take time away from work

The solution is certainly not to reduce maternity leave. Rather, the solution is simply to expect men and women to contribute equally (or roughly equally) at home and at the very least create a policy environment that allows them to make that choice.

FRAUD: FIVE CASE STUDIES

Let's now look at some of the big cases of bad ethics with a focus on emerging markets. These are all cases where there were clear breaches of the law but also where basic ethical principles (and their application) would have prevented significant loss. These are some of the biggest emerging market corporate scandals that have occurred over the past decade.

CASE STUDY 1:
TONGYANG GROUP
(SOUTH KOREA, 2013)

The Tongyang Group scandal, also known as the Tongyang Group financial fraud case, unfolded in South Korea in 2013.[38] It involved the prominent conglomerate Tongyang Group and its subsidiaries, Tongyang Securities and Tongyang Cement, which were found to have engaged in fraudulent practices and misleading financial reporting. The company had inflated its profits, concealed losses and engaged in unethical financial practices. The scandal led to the company's bankruptcy and caused significant financial losses for investors.

The scandal came to light when Tongyang Group's subsidiaries faced severe financial difficulties and struggled to repay their debts. It was revealed that Tongyang Securities had engaged in irregular and fraudulent activities to cover up losses and inflate its financial performance.

One of the key aspects of the scandal was the misuse of client funds. Tongyang Securities had allegedly used customer deposits to fund its own speculative investments and cover losses incurred in its securities trading operations. This violated regulatory requirements and jeopardized the financial security of the firm's clients.

Furthermore, Tongyang Securities was found to have manipulated its financial statements by overstating profits and concealing losses. It employed accounting tricks, such as fictitious transactions and circular financing, to artificially inflate its financial position and mislead investors and creditors.

The fallout from the scandal was significant. Tongyang Securities faced liquidity issues and struggled to repay its debts, leading to a credit crunch and financial distress within the Tongyang Group as a whole. The scandal had wider implications for the financial sector in South Korea, as it raised concerns about the integrity and transparency of the country's financial institutions.

The South Korean authorities launched investigations into the Tongyang Group, with the Financial Supervisory Service and the prosecution playing pivotal roles. They sought to uncover the full extent of the fraudulent activities, hold responsible individuals accountable, and restore stability and trust in the financial system.

As a result of the investigations, several high-ranking executives and officials from Tongyang Group were arrested and faced criminal charges for their involvement in the fraud. The authorities also implemented measures to strengthen regulations and oversight in the financial sector, aiming to prevent similar incidents in the future.

The Tongyang Group scandal had a profound impact on the South Korean business landscape. It led to increased scrutiny of corporate governance practices and financial reporting standards across the country. The scandal prompted calls for improved transparency, accountability and ethical conduct in the business sector.

Efforts were made to address the financial fallout from the scandal and protect the interests of investors and creditors. Tongyang Securities underwent restructuring and sought external support to stabilize its financial position. Creditors of Tongyang Group negotiated debt repayment plans and restructuring agreements to mitigate losses.

The Tongyang Group scandal serves as a reminder of the importance of robust corporate governance, ethical business practices and regulatory oversight. It highlights the need for effective measures to prevent fraud, protect investors, and ensure the stability and integrity of financial institutions. The scandal led to reforms and heightened awareness of the importance of transparency, accountability and risk management within the South Korean business environment.

CASE STUDY 2:
PETROBRAS
(BRAZIL, 2014)

The Petrobras scandal, also known as Operation Car Wash, was a corruption scheme involving the state-owned oil company Petrobras in Brazil.[39] The scandal, which broke in 2014, exposed a vast network of bribes and kickbacks involving politicians, Petrobras executives and construction companies. It resulted in numerous arrests, the impeachment of the Brazilian president, and significant economic and political repercussions.

The scandal came to light when investigations by Brazilian federal police revealed that Petrobras executives had been receiving bribes from construction companies in exchange for awarding them lucrative contracts. These companies would overcharge Petrobras for their services and funnel a portion of the excess funds back to the executives and political parties involved.

The bribes and kickbacks were estimated to amount to billions of dollars over several years, with the money being used for personal enrichment, political campaign financing and illicit purposes. The scheme involved a complex network of intermediaries, money launderers and offshore accounts to hide the illicit funds.

As the investigations progressed, it became clear that the corruption extended beyond Petrobras. Numerous politicians from various parties, including high-ranking members of the ruling Workers' Party, were implicated in the scandal. The revelations shook the political establishment in Brazil, eroding public trust and leading to widespread protests and demands for accountability.

Operation Car Wash, led by federal judge Sergio Moro and later continued by prosecutors in the Operation Car Wash task force, became one of the largest and most complex investigations in Brazilian history. It involved cooperation with international authorities, including the USA and Switzerland, as the money-laundering operations spanned multiple jurisdictions.

The scandal had significant economic repercussions for Petrobras and Brazil as a whole. Petrobras, being a major player in the Brazilian economy, saw its stock value plummet, and its ability to invest and secure financing was severely impacted. The company had to resubmit its financial statements, revealing massive losses and impairments due to the inflated costs associated with the corrupt contracts.

The Petrobras scandal also had broader implications for the Brazilian economy. The revelations of widespread corruption and the subsequent political instability led to a decline in investor confidence, capital flight and a contraction in economic activity. The country slipped into a deep recession, exacerbating social inequality and unemployment rates.

The investigations and legal proceedings resulting from the scandal were officially ongoing until February 2021. Many high-profile politicians and executives were arrested, prosecuted and sentenced for their involvement. The scandal also prompted reforms in Brazil's political and business sectors, including measures to enhance transparency, anti-corruption laws and enforcement mechanisms.

The Petrobras scandal served as a wake-up call for Brazil, highlighting the urgent need for systemic changes to combat corruption and strengthen accountability.

It demonstrated the intertwining of political and business interests and the detrimental effects of corrupt practices on a national scale. The investigations and the ongoing fight against corruption contributed to a growing awareness of the need for transparency and integrity in public and private institutions, not only in Brazil but also globally.

CASE STUDY 3:
1MALAYSIA DEVELOPMENT BERHAD
(MALAYSIA, 2015)

The 1Malaysia Development Berhad (1MDB) scandal involved the misappropriation of billions of dollars from a large Malaysian state investment fund.[40] It led to the downfall of former Malaysian prime minister Najib Razak and implicated high-ranking officials and international financiers. Overall, the scandal highlighted the extent of corruption and financial misconduct within the Malaysian government.

1MDB was established in 2009 as a strategic development fund with the goal of promoting economic growth in Malaysia. However, over the years, it became embroiled in a web of fraudulent activities and contracts. The scandal began to unravel in 2015 when reports emerged suggesting that approximately $700 million from 1MDB had been transferred into Najib Razak's personal bank accounts.

As investigations progressed, it was revealed that a staggering amount of money, estimated to be around $4.5 billion, had been misappropriated from 1MDB. The funds were allegedly used for personal gain, political financing and extravagant purchases, including luxury real estate, artworks, jewellery and even (ironically) financing Hollywood films such as *The Wolf of Wall Street* (2013).

The scandal implicated several individuals and entities, including high-ranking officials, businesspeople and international financiers. One prominent figure was Jho Low, a Malaysian financier who played a central role in orchestrating the fraudulent activities. Low was known for his lavish lifestyle and connections to influential figures around the world. He allegedly used complex financial transactions and shell companies to siphon money from 1MDB.

The investigations into the 1MDB scandal were led by authorities from various countries, including Malaysia, the USA and Switzerland. They revealed a complex network of money laundering and illicit financial activities spanning multiple jurisdictions. Assets worth billions of dollars were frozen or seized, including luxury real estate, yachts and artwork, as authorities sought to recover the misappropriated funds.

The fallout from the scandal was significant. It led to political upheaval in Malaysia, with Najib Razak facing mounting pressure to step down as prime minister. In 2018, Najib was charged with multiple counts of corruption and money laundering related to the 1MDB scandal.

The 1MDB scandal also had economic consequences for Malaysia. The misappropriation of funds and the subsequent investigation raised concerns about the country's financial stability and credibility among investors. It led to credit rating downgrades, a decline in investor confidence and significant losses for companies and individuals associated with 1MDB. Here the poor and very unethical decisions of a few individuals impacted millions of people.

Efforts to recover the misappropriated funds and hold the individuals involved accountable continue to this day. The Malaysian government has pursued legal actions to recover assets and funds linked to the scandal, both domestically and internationally. Cooperation with foreign jurisdictions has been crucial in facilitating these efforts.

The 1MDB scandal serves as a stark reminder of the far-reaching consequences of corruption and financial misconduct. It highlights the need for stronger governance, transparency and accountability in both public and private institutions. The investigations and legal actions surrounding the scandal set a precedent for tackling financial fraud and corruption, not only in Malaysia but also globally. The application of a simple set of ethical standards would have helped leaders avoid this major case of fraud.

CASE STUDY 4:
STEINHOFF INTERNATIONAL
(SOUTH AFRICA, 2017)

Steinhoff International, a South African multinational retail holding company, faced a major scandal in 2017 related to accounting irregularities.[41] The company's former CEO, Markus Jooste, resigned, and it was revealed that there had been substantial overstatements of profits and asset values. The scandal led to significant losses for investors and a decline in the company's stock value. This was a serious case of failed leadership.

The scandal is considered one of the largest corporate accounting fraud cases in South African history.

The scandal began when Steinhoff announced in December 2017 that it had uncovered accounting irregularities. It was revealed that the company had overstated its profits and assets for several years, creating a deeply misleading picture of its financial health. The irregularities were estimated to amount to billions of dollars. Investors had been misled, and the revelation triggered a rapid decline in Steinhoff's share price.

As investigations unfolded, it became apparent that the accounting irregularities were pervasive and complex, with many of them relating to contractual issues. The company had used various accounting techniques and off-balance-sheet entities to inflate profits and hide debt. These practices involved fictitious transactions, inflated asset values and the manipulation of financial statements to present a more positive financial position.

The key figure at the centre of the scandal was Markus Jooste, the former CEO of Steinhoff. Jooste had played a significant role in orchestrating the fraudulent activities and concealing the true financial state of the company. He resigned just before the scandal broke and subsequent investigations have been focused on his actions and the involvement of other high-level executives.

The fallout from the Steinhoff scandal was significant. Shareholders and investors experienced substantial financial losses as the company's share price plummeted. Steinhoff's credit rating was downgraded, making it difficult for the company to secure financing. Legal actions and shareholder lawsuits were initiated against the company and its executives, seeking compensation for the losses incurred.

The scandal also had broader implications for South Africa's economy and reputation. Steinhoff was one of the country's largest employers and had significant international operations. The revelations of widespread financial misconduct raised concerns about corporate governance and accountability within South African companies. They also led to a loss of confidence in the country's investment climate and contributed to negative perceptions of the broader business environment. These knock-on consequences impacted thousands of people in (and outside) the country.

In response to the scandal, various regulatory bodies and authorities launched investigations into Steinhoff's affairs. These included the South African Reserve Bank, the Financial Sector Conduct Authority and regulatory bodies in other jurisdictions where the company operated. The investigations aimed to uncover the full extent of the accounting irregularities, hold those responsible accountable and implement measures to prevent similar occurrences in the future.

Steinhoff has undertaken significant efforts to address the fallout from the scandal. The company has implemented various restructuring measures, including asset sales and debt renegotiations, to stabilize its financial position. It has also cooperated with authorities and initiated legal actions against former executives and business associates involved in the fraud.

The Steinhoff International scandal serves as a reminder of the importance of transparency, ethical conduct and robust corporate governance in business. It highlights the need for stronger oversight and regulation to prevent and detect financial misconduct.

It was the clear responsibility of the numerous leaders involved to apply an ethical framework that might have avoided these disastrous outcomes. The aftermath of the scandal has spurred discussions and reforms around corporate accountability, auditing practices, and investor protection in South Africa and beyond.

CASE STUDY 5:
NIRAV MODI
(INDIA, 2018)

The Nirav Modi scam, which came to light in 2018, is one of the largest banking frauds in the history of India.[42] It involved renowned Indian jeweller Nirav Modi and his associates defrauding Punjab National Bank (PNB), one of India's largest state-owned banks, of billions of dollars through counterfeit transactions and manipulation of the banking system.

The scam unfolded when PNB discovered unauthorized transactions carried out by Modi's companies, specifically his flagship firm, Firestar Diamond International, and its subsidiaries. It was revealed that Modi and his associates had fraudulently obtained credit guarantees from PNB using phony letters of undertaking (LoUs) and foreign letters of credit (FLCs).

LoUs and FLCs are instruments used in international trade to facilitate credit between banks. In this case, Modi's companies would submit fraudulent LoUs and FLCs to PNB, which allowed them to obtain funds from overseas banks. These guarantees were issued without proper collateral or due diligence, and the scam went undetected for several years.

The fraudulent transactions were orchestrated through a complex network of companies and subsidiaries spread across multiple jurisdictions. Money obtained through these fraudulent means was used for personal expenses, to fund Modi's jewellery business and for other undisclosed purposes.

The scam's magnitude was staggering, with the total amount involved estimated to be around US$2 billion. The funds obtained fraudulently were primarily used to obtain diamonds and other luxury goods for Modi's jewellery business, as well as to fund a lavish lifestyle.

Once the fraud was uncovered, a massive investigation was launched by Indian authorities, including the Central Bureau of Investigation and the Directorate of Enforcement. These bodies initiated criminal proceedings, freezing assets and issuing arrest warrants for Modi, his family members and other individuals involved in the scam.

Modi, along with his family, fled India before the scam came to light and sought refuge in various countries, including the United Kingdom. The Indian authorities initiated his extradition process, which resulted in a high-profile legal battle in the UK courts. After a prolonged legal process, Modi was finally extradited to India in 2021 to face charges related to the scam.

The Modi scam exposed significant shortcomings in India's banking system, particularly related to risk management, internal controls and oversight mechanisms. It prompted a reassessment of the country's banking regulations and processes to prevent similar frauds in the future. The scam also highlighted the need for stronger enforcement of anti-money-laundering and anti-corruption laws.

The impact of the scam was not limited to the banking sector. It had broader implications for investor confidence, the gems and jewellery industry, and India's reputation as a business destination. The scam raised questions about corporate governance, lending practices, and the nexus between businesses and banks in India.

Efforts to recover the defrauded funds and seize assets are ongoing. The Indian authorities have auctioned off Modi's seized assets, including luxury cars, jewellery and artwork, to repay a portion of the defrauded amount. Legal proceedings against the accused individuals are still in progress, with the hope of recovering a larger portion of the defrauded funds.

The Nirav Modi scam serves as a stark reminder of the importance of robust banking systems, effective risk management, and strong regulatory oversight in preventing fraud and protecting the interests of depositors and stakeholders. It has prompted a re-evaluation of procedures, regulations and corporate governance practices in India's banking sector and highlighted the need for enhanced vigilance and transparency to safeguard the financial system.

CHAPTER 8

ENJOY THE JOURNEY

BY YUSUF

When Matt and I set out to write this book, we had a clear purpose – to help people build careers they can be proud of. Naturally, we assumed that such a pursuit is desirable to the average person as it can serve as a means to realize a host of ambitions, beyond just earning a living. This includes amassing wealth, attaining positions of leadership and making a positive change in the world.

But have you ever considered what the underlying motivation or driving force behind your ambitions are? Why do you want the things you want? I think you will agree that any rational, or reasonably intelligent person strives to attain a state of happiness, contentment and overall well-being (mental, emotional, physical and spiritual). So, it's logical to assume that our personal and professional endeavours are fundamentally geared towards cultivating happiness and a sense of well-being.

This philosophical assertion may appear out of place among the practical advice provided throughout this book, but it is perhaps the most important perspective to maintain along your journey towards professional success. It should also inform the decisions you make throughout your career. Unfortunately, stories of accomplished professionals who are miserable, unwell and languishing in the wake of broken relationships are all too common. Therefore, this book would be incomplete if we neglected to provide some advice on how to achieve and maintain a sense of happiness and well-being while navigating your professional career. It's a balance that can be surprisingly difficult to get right, especially when you are ambitious and want the best out of life and your professional career.

Unfortunately, there's no magic formula or silver bullet, but there are principles and perspectives that I have found to be effective. These have been borne out of my own research and experience as someone who has a keen interest in understanding the drivers of human happiness and how to optimize mental, emotional and physical well-being. The insights shared in this chapter have been enriched by the wisdom of many people I've engaged with – the majority of whom have not only attained significant corporate success but also radiate genuine contentment and happiness. Let's get stuck in!

FIND YOUR OWN FLOW

The level of social connectivity and integration we experience today is nothing short of mind-blowing. Twenty years ago, our social circles were mostly confined to people whom we physically met. Today we can connect with near countless numbers of people from almost anywhere on the planet, instantly, and across the full spectrum of society – from ordinary individuals to the most famous people on the planet. We might not actually meet most of them, but we can still be part of their lives by liking and commenting on their posts, whether it's about their outfits, the food they eat, the places they go, or their seemingly never ending successes (failures? Not so much!). I won't go into the whole debate about whether the age of (over)sharing and social media is good or bad, but what's clear is that we're living in an era where our views are heavily influenced by the mindset of others – the 'mob' if you will. I would even venture further to say that there is now a global 'gold standard' of what happiness and success looks like – and we're all kind of chasing it.

Social media is flooded with images of effortlessly put-together people who seem to have mastered the art of excelling in every facet of life. They rise with the sun, head to the gym before work, seal mega-deals, all while maintaining impeccable style and indulging in picture-perfect meals. Even their seemingly mundane moments hold an aesthetic charm that's curated to perfection. While the irony is that most of what we see on social media is actually highlight reels only, it's no surprise that many of us have felt like hopeless under achievers at some point or another.

Okay, I'm being a bit cynical, I know. But I want to make a point; ALL the apparent success you see on social media is just noise. Don't let it distract you from your own path.

I spent a big part of my twenties searching for mentors and voraciously reading self-help books hoping to find a model for success that I could replicate. I was disappointed and disillusioned when I was not able to find one at the time. Instead, over time, I learned a more profound life lesson: following your own distinct path is the ultimate key to long-term happiness and success. This is a unique and individualized experience for each and every one of us. While we can leverage our integrated way of living and interacting to learn from those around us, we must own and charter our own course in the context of the circumstances of our lives. This will require you to adjust your priorities accordingly so that you are able to respond appropriately to the circumstances you find yourself in. Ultimately the real magic lies in forging our own way, and this will require you to adjust your priorities accordingly so that you are able to respond to the circumstances you find yourself in.

What does this mean in practical terms? Well, it boils down to two fundamental questions: 'Who am I?' and 'What is my purpose?'

Stay with me as we dive deep, for the answers to these existential questions which will act as a North Star guiding you through the unpredictable, and most likely, non-linear voyage of your professional journey – one that's bound to be both demanding and rewarding, while hopefully remaining fun and meaningful.

WHO AM I?

The question 'Who am I?' plagued me for a significant portion of my adult life. I am perhaps not alone in this as it is a question that has challenged many, from Socrates to Gandhi to Mandela. I'm a fourth-generation South African-born male of Indian descent – my identity is a mix of many elements. But who am I at the core? What truly defines me? Honestly, I still don't have all the answers, but what I do know is what I stand for – my values. These values provide the framework through which I have chosen to given some colour and substance to this age-old question.

Now, when we talk of values, elements around morality and ethics invariably pop into our minds – integrity, honesty, courage, selflessness (you get where I am going with this). While these are important, the values I am referring to go beyond these fundamentals (or table stakes, if you will). I am referring to your own personal values above and beyond these baseline values (which are no doubt prerequisites for functioning society). What do you like? What do you dislike?

What truly inspires you? What excites you? Answering these seemingly simple questions is more challenging than it appears. I mean answering them at a deep, intrinsic level, free from the influence of religious, social or other systems seeking to guide us. Having the courage to not only explore these answers but also shape a life that matches these values will help you see your path more clearly. And these answers will serve as a solid foundation from which confidence and self-belief will grow – qualities that are just as important, if not more important, than any skill or ability you can develop.

Know that these values will evolve over time, too. What serves you today may suffocate you tomorrow. Your values will also evolve as you absorb new information about life through the process of actually living. This evolution is entirely natural, and I would even argue, essential for growth and development. But I have learned that while there is an element of change that happens at a more surface level, deep down there is an inherent component to who you are that's part of your very DNA. Cherish and safeguard this for it contributes to your unique identity and is what set you apart.

WHAT IS MY PURPOSE?

We explored purpose at the beginning of this book and now we revisit it as we near the end.

I spent a considerable amount of time grappling with the idea of purpose, hoping that it would serve as a guiding light for the trajectory of my life. Yet, reality has shown me that much like your sense of self, your purpose evolves over time. What is important is to spend some time thinking about what your purpose is at various points in your life so you can adjust your focus and priorities accordingly.

For example, there may be a period when your purpose is to gain as much knowledge and experience within your field as possible with the next five years – a common and sensible objective, especially early in your career. This means that other things become less important in your pursuit of this purpose or goal. For instance, you may receive a very lucrative job offer that, while tempting, would divert you from gaining the skills and experience you're aiming for. What do you choose – go for the job with the fat paycheck or stay put for a better chance at achieving your skill-building goal? This process will repeat itself many times throughout your life, so having a clearly articulated purpose for each period provides the framework you need to navigate and think through decisions like these.

The fundamental aim of answering both of these questions – 'Who am I?' and 'What is my purpose?' – is to develop a mindset that is a true representation of your authentic self, untainted by external influences, societal pressures or fleeting trends. This will guide the definition of your purpose and serve as a guiding light, both in your personal and professional life. From my experience, it is the cultivation of this mindset that serves to differentiate those who are good from those who become truly great.

KEEP THINGS IN PERSPECTIVE

There's no easy way to say this, and I would be doing you a great disservice if I attempted to euphemize these facts – life is often difficult, failures are inevitable and things rarely work out exactly the way you want them to. To navigate this reality, flexibility, adaptability and a willingness to consider various perspectives are key. Keeping things in perspective means examining the circumstances you encounter through more than a single lens or angle – and beyond your immediate viewpoint. This will allow for a more holistic understanding of the (sometimes prickly!) situations you might face.

Here is a personal example: early in my career, I was nominated to be part of a cohort of high-performing analysts who were seconded to work on a large-scale transformational project. We were told categorically that this project would be the conduit through which we would be fast-tracked to middle management and set on a path towards executive leadership, well ahead of our peers. We felt like masters of the universe, cocooned in a bubble of invincibility and fantasizing about the lifestyle that corporate success at a young age could provide.

Towards the end of the same year – 2007 – capitalism's insatiable greed got the better of it. This culminated in an event known today as the Global Financial Crisis. A wave of panic swept across the world and millions lost their jobs. Our cohort was not spared, and so, instead of being fast-tracked along the path towards corporate success, I was retrenched. I was gutted and remember feeling like my life had been tuned upside down. The vision I had for my career, along with my dreams, were pinned to a plan that had now gone up in smoke!

In the midst of feeling sorry for myself, a friend gave me some blunt advice: "Yusuf, you need to get over it. It's only a job!" The words landed like a slap in the face, but also served as a wake-up call. This was just the perspective I needed – the jolt to get me off my ass – and it made me realize that I was placing far too much importance on just one part of my life. Sure, it mattered, but it was only one part of the whole, and deriving such a large chunk of my self-worth and happiness from it was absurd. Since then, I have kept this perspective at the front of my mind, and it continues to serve me whenever I find myself dealing with difficult people and challenging situations. Tough times are inevitable, but keeping things in perspective makes all the difference.

Another lesson that I learned during this time was the importance of having not only a 'plan B,' but also plans and strategies that can pivot and adapt in response to unexpected twists.In the book *How Will You Measure Your Life?*, Clayton M. Christensen calls these "emergent strategies."[43] These are shifts in our game plan that we can make to respond to unexpected events that throw us off course. This is important because there will be many instances where things are not going to go according to plan. Instead of wallowing in self-pity, embrace a flexible mindset. Anticipate that your plans might require recalibration due to unforeseen challenges. The path towards happiness and success is imperfect and you must embrace this imperfection – something that many high achievers struggle with. Expect detours and unexpected hurdles, but also be ready for growth opportunities and unforeseen developments. Maintain a long-term vision, but be open to adjusting your path frequently.

HEALTH

The stresses and anxieties of navigating tough situations and managing uncertainty can have a huge impact on your health (mental, physical and emotional). I cannot overstress the importance of taking good care of your body and mind. There are no magic formulas or pills for staying healthy (though an entire industry exists to tell you otherwise). Remember, those models with perfectly chiselled abs who promote fad diets and designer-label gym gear are paid to look like that because that is their full-time job! The fact that you are reading this book probably means that you are unlikely to be a professional fitness model, and you, like the rest of us, get paid to do other things. Those other things need to find a place in the context of your life, but so does your eating and exercising regimen. Being conscious of the food you eat and exercising regularly are imperative. If you are not physically well, it's going to be tough to sustain a successful career.

Taking care of your mental and emotional health is just as important. I've have found that meditation and practising mindfulness, along with making sure I get a few minutes of sunshine and fresh air (a walk outside can work wonders!), is helpful in managing stress and anxiety. Of course, these techniques might not suit everyone, so explore what works best for you. The long and short of it is this – make the time to look after your body and mind, and be cognisant of the fact that you need to manage the impact that your career has on your health. It is senseless to achieve a successful career only to have sacrificed your health along the way.

RELATIONSHIPS

In the midst of any ambitious pursuit, it's easy to lose sight of what truly matters – like our health and relationships. When the allure of corporate success beckons, the non-stop grind can consume us, overshadowing the need to nurture personal relationships and spend quality time with the important people in your life. Don't let this happen to you. We are fundamentally social creatures, and our relationships are the cornerstone of lasting happiness. And so, amidst all of your career advances, make a conscious effort to invest time and energy into personal bonds and connections. Even as the demands of your busy job intensify, make sure you carve out the time to build, maintain and nurture your relationships. To do this, you may need to set clear boundaries. This might seem daunting, especially in work environments where long hours are normalized. Be firm with your boundaries, regardless, or at least as far as is reasonable. Of course, there will be times when working overtime or putting in extra hours is necessary and even commendable.

However, allowing this to become a perpetual norm can be detrimental, not only to your well-being but also to your relationships. Constantly sacrificing time meant for family or friends in favour of work is unsustainable and can lead to strained relationships and burnout. Striking a balance between dedication to your career and nurturing your personal relationships is the key for your long-term success and inner peace. Remember that prioritizing your personal time and relationships isn't just about happiness – it may very well improve your chance of attaining success in your career as healthy relationships and a happy home will enrich you with a sense of joy, support and fulfillment.success because your relationships will have provided you with happiness, support and fulfilment along the way.

THE JOURNEY

The journey to success is often a path filled with both highs and lows. When striving for greatness, careers seldom follow a clear, straightforward trajectory. It's common to lose sight of this reality and feel disheartened, not recognizing the positive trend that consistent effort creates over time.

Figure 13 demonstrates the relationship between success (a proxy for career progression, money, etc.) and time.

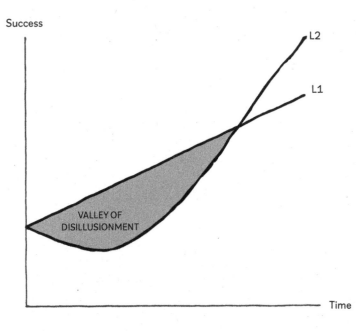

FIGURE 13
LINEAR VS NON-LINEAR SUCCESS

Line 1 (L1) is the consistent, predictable path: you enter into a job as a graduate and stick around for the next 20–30 years, notching up annual increases and promotions along the way. The linear correlation between success and time plays out like a well-orchestrated symphony (assuming you've met or exceeded expectations along the way). Most of the L1 people I know fit into similar moulds – predictable, risk averse, dependable – and often have a well-defined plan and an early understanding of their career aspirations and goals. They also make informed decisions that align with their chosen trajectory, creating a sense of security and dependability in their professional endeavours.

Without a doubt, these qualities and characteristics are commendable, and I have always admired and even envied people like this because my career has been the complete opposite. To L1 people I would only say two things: (1) While a clear plan can be hugely advantageous, make sure that you periodically reevaluate your goals to make sure that they still align with your passions and aspirations. (2) Consider embracing calculated risks from time to time. These risks can inject fresh energy into your journey and open doors to unexpected opportunities. Remember, while predictability offers security, venturing slightly off the beaten path can foster growth and new horizons.

Line 2 (L2) represents a non-linear trajectory, closer to my own experience. Line 2 people often embody a distinct blend of curiosity and risk-taking. They tend to veer away from the conventional path and are more comfortable with uncertainty. While L2 is arguably the less 'stable' path to take, the good news is that many successful people have also gone down this road. It is, however, important to note that in the short to medium term, the 'line to success' tends to dip downward. This can feel like a 'shaky start,' especially in the early years of experimentation and (sensible) risk-taking and can lead to a gap between you and more conventional peers.

As this gap seemingly grows wider (again, in the short to medium term) it creates a 'valley of disillusionment' marked by uncertainty and doubt. During this phase, you might question your choices and compare yourself to your L1 peers, wondering if you will ever make it or be destined for the history books as a hopeless underachiever. Amid the uncertainty, remember to reflect on your progress and reframe your mistakes as lessons. Seek support from mentors and peers to gain fresh perspectives. Stay adaptable, adjusting your strategies without abandoning your goals. And, above all, practise self-compassion, understanding that setbacks don't define you. Keep moving forward with determination whilst trusting in the process, knowing this phase is a stepping stone to your personal and professional growth. Remember that persistent effort can yield success beyond your initial expectations. Maintain this perspective, especially when things don't go to plan – a reality that's bound to happen.

TRUST IN THE PROCESS

There are two types of ambitious people in the corporate world – those who know exactly where are they are heading and have a solid plan in place to help them to get there (like L1 friends), and those who have only a vague idea about their future and don't have much clarity about the things they want, but know that they also want to succeed in some meaningful way.

I am part of the latter group. As I mentioned, earlier in my career, I often found myself feeling somewhat purposeless because I lacked the certainty about the future that some of my colleagues had. I must admit that this bugged me for a long time, and I sometimes felt positively sick with anxiety about not knowing where I was heading or what my professional goals were. But as time went on, I realized that not knowing exactly where you are heading, especially when you are starting out, is perfectly fine. If you focus more on the process and less on the outcome, and work hard while maintaining a strong sense of optimism, your professional path will become clearer as you progress.

Early in my career, I had the good fortune of being mentored by the CEO of a media conglomerate a few years ago (it's worth mentioning that this was made possible only through putting myself out there and networking!). During one of our conversations, while I was in a state of professional purposelessness, I asked him how he had become a CEO – had he known from an early age that he wanted to be the CEO of a media business? He told me that he had no idea that he would end up where he was when he started out. What he did know was that he wanted to be the best at whatever it was that he was doing. So, he honed his focus on the projects that were right in front on him, year after year, until the path to the coveted C-suite materialized.

This impressed on me the value of focusing on the thing I can control – the process. It taught me that a career is more a journey that needs to be experienced fully than it is a series of discrete destinations that we need to race towards. Crucially, it reminded me that even some of the most accomplished people in the corporate world begin their careers without a fixed destination in mind! So, enjoy the ride and trust that if you persevere, with a bit of luck, you too can achieve the professional success you desire and have a life filled with meaning, happiness and overall well-being. Matt and I wholeheartedly believe that the advice set forth in this book will help steer you there. Armed with the knowledge woven through these pages and shaped by the perspectives we've laid bare, along with the flex-ibility to learn and incorporate fresh insights along the way, your odds of success will soar. Like everyone who tries to contribute towards the betterment of the world and society, we have aimed to move the conversation forward by blending our own unique thoughts and ideas with some age-old wisdom. We now hand over the baton to you and ask that you take the ideas in this book to the next level. Go forth and conquer.

Here's to your remarkable journey of cracking corporate and beyond.

AFTERWORD: A NOTE ON AI

BY YUSUF

As we draw to the end of writing this book, a significant technological revolution is unfolding. As we stand at the dawn of a new era, technology is shaping our lives in unprecedented ways. Among these technological advancements, artificial intelligence (AI) stands out as a force that will undoubtedly transform our careers and the world we live in.

With the widespread deployment of generative pre-trained transformers (GPTs), a key advancement in AI, many of us are beginning to realize that the AI revolution is no longer some distant concept or science fiction, but a tangible reality that will shape our lives and careers in ways we are still in the process of fully grasping. With this in mind, Matt and I felt compelled to share some thoughts on the exciting potential AI holds for you as you prepare to enter or progress in the corporate world and navigate your professional journey.

The AI revolution is ushering us into an era where awe-inspiring advancements in technology will drive a multitude of developments with far-reaching implications. It has the potential to impact every facet of human existence, instigating a radical overhaul of industries, restructuring economies and bringing about paradigm shifts in the ways we live, socialize and, most relevant to readers of this book, build our careers. Such a dramatic shift can understandably be overwhelming, evoking exhilaration, anticipation, trepidation and perhaps even an undercurrent of fear – especially for individuals contemplating their career trajectories. This fear, stemming from uncertainty and a fear of upheaval and obsolescence, is a common sentiment that has surfaced throughout human history whenever we have been on the brink of revolutionary innovation.

Today, we stand at the cusp of a similar transformation and face familiar anxieties about job displacement and skill redundancy, forcing us to face up to some existential questions. Some that come to mind include:

- What will be the impact of AI on my chosen profession?
- Will I be replaced by a robot?
- Which professions will persist?
- What new roles will surface?
- How can I equip myself for a future fraught with unpredictability?

While we don't have the answers, we don't believe they will be as bleak as some might fear.

In the face of such uncertainty, some people's instinct might be to retreat from the advancing tide of AI. Yet history has consistently demonstrated that periods of monumental change are fertile grounds for immense, once-in-lifetime opportunities. Whether it was the advent of the printing press, the Industrial Revolution or the Digital Age, periods of great change have laid the foundations for platforms that serve to accelerate our progression towards a better world.

Consider the 15th century, when Johannes Gutenberg unleashed the power of the printing press. The scribes, fearing for their livelihoods, found that the invention didn't eliminate their profession; it redefined it. They metamorphosed into editors, publishers and journalists, continuing to contribute meaningfully in a world transformed by the printed word.

Similarly, during the Industrial Revolution, traditional artisans, resistant to change, found that society didn't crumble but adapted, evolved and flourished.

Over time these artisans adjusted their skills to fit the swiftly changing landscape, just as the scribes had done before them. These transformative periods are now hailed as key catalysts for substantial societal and economic advancement.

These examples offer a crucial lesson and serve to endorse the point that while disruption heralds a period of uncertainty and apprehension, it also uncovers opportunities for those prepared to adapt, grow and leverage the emerging tools of their time.

While it is important to acknowledge the potential risks and dangers of the misuse of AI, it is equally crucial to recognize the immense promise it holds for transforming various aspects of our lives. AI has the power to make a hugely positive impact on numerous key areas, such as healthcare, climate change mitigation, education, transportation and business efficiency – pushing us towards a more sustainable, equitable future.

So, it's crucial to see AI not as a force of destruction intent on wiping out jobs but rather as an ally that serves as a flywheel – a leverage point to enhance human potential, equipping us to tackle complex problems more efficiently. Tools, from the humble sticks used by early humans to the advanced AI algorithms of today, amplify our capabilities; they don't make us redundant. AI will indeed transform the economic landscape and reshape the job market, and *some* careers as we know them may indeed cease to exist. However, much like during the eras of the Gutenberg press and the Industrial Revolution, when the scribes and the artisans adapted to their changing eras, it is incumbent upon us to adapt, evolve and seize the new tools within our grasp and carve out our unique niches in the age of AI.

What, then, will be our guiding principle as we chart the unexplored territory of this uncertain but magnificent new world? It lies in the timeless wisdom demonstrated by historical trailblazers such as Ibn Battuta, Leonardo da Vinci, Ada Lovelace, Marie Curie, Albert Einstein and Steve Jobs: the audacity to follow your curiosity. It is this insatiable desire to explore, to understand and to create that has propelled us forward throughout history. It will lead you down paths unseen, towards the discovery of ideas unimagined. It will help you to see not just what is but what could be. It will push you to learn, unlearn and relearn, adapting in stride with the changing times.

Consider the story of Ibn Battuta, a 14th-century Moroccan explorer who traversed the length and breadth of the Medieval world, driven by nothing more than an insatiable curiosity and a desire to learn, daring to question the familiar. He ventured into unknown territories, pushed boundaries, and shared knowledge about diverse cultures and societies, contributing significantly to our understanding of the Medieval world. His curiosity was his compass, and it guided him through unfamiliar terrains and uncharted territories, creating an interconnectedness among distant societies, fostering mutual respect and understanding, and laying the groundwork for the globalized world we know today.

Leonardo da Vinci, the ultimate Renaissance polymath, merged art and science with insatiable curiosity. His masterpieces, such as the *Mona Lisa* and visionary sketches of flying machines, left an enduring impact. Da Vinci's artistry redefined portraiture, while his ideas for flying machines and anatomical studies foreshadowed advancements in aviation and medicine. His legacy exemplifies the transformative power of curiosity, art and science in shaping human progress.

Ada Lovelace, the world's first computer programmer, chose to focus on a field few women ventured into during her time. Her fascination with computational mechanics led her to envision the foundation of modern programming long before computers existed.

Marie Curie, driven by insatiable curiosity, revolutionized our understanding of radioactivity. Her fearless pursuit of knowledge and ground-breaking research shaped physics, chemistry and medicine, leaving an enduring impact on scientific exploration and forever changing our understanding of the natural world.

Similarly, Albert Einstein's intense curiosity about the fundamental laws of the universe led to his theory of relativity, forever changing our understanding of space, time and gravity.

And of course Steve Jobs, a visionary entrepreneur, who revolutionized the tech landscape and our daily lives through innovative products, famously championed the significance of embracing curiosity during his 2005 commencement speech at Stanford University

Each of these individuals, in their unique ways, navigated the complexities and uncertainties of their times by following their curiosity and leveraging the tools of their era. In this way, they made meaningful, enduring impacts on the world.

In a rapidly evolving world driven by AI, our careers are not fixed paths but journeys of constant adaptation and transformation. Curiosity makes us flexible, and helps us embrace new ideas and view challenges as opportunities for learning and growth. It will serve as our compass, guiding us through the unknown and keeping us relevant.

Our advice is to educate yourself about AI – learn how it works, and explore the myriad ways it can be leveraged. Recognize the immense power you hold in shaping your future and career with AI. Never underestimate the influence you can have. Remember that even the greatest achievements, like humanity's first journey to the Moon, began with small, exploratory steps.

Embrace this new frontier and leverage the tools at your disposal. Seize the possibilities, explore uncharted territories and leave your mark on the canvas of our AI-driven world. Your journey is just beginning, and the impact you can make is boundless. The future holds incredible promise, and it is within your grasp to shape it. With your own unique skills and knowledge, coupled with AI as a powerful tool at your disposal, you hold the keys to cracking the code to success in your career.

The AI revolution is not merely about machines – it is about the human spirit that dreams, innovates and pioneers. It is about *you*. So, be passionately curious. Explore, question, innovate. Let your curiosity guide you through this era of transformation. Let it lead you to new ideas, new solutions and new ways of making a positive impact.

In the words of Einstein, "I have no special talent. I am only passionately curious."[44] Remember that as we journey into this brave new world. Be passionately curious. Be courageous. Be ready to shape and be shaped by this AI revolution. The future awaits, and it is ripe with possibilities.

REFERENCES

1. "Corporate" (*Cambridge Dictionary*), accessed 28 June 2023, https://dictionary.cambridge.org/dictionary/english/corporate.

2. "Business School Rankings: Executive Education Custom 2023" (*Financial Times*), last modified 21 May 2023, https://rankings.ft.com/rankings/2945/executive-education-custom-2023.

3. See https://www.enneagraminstitute.com.

4. See https://www.themyersbriggs.com.

5. Stein and Swan (2019); https://swanpsych.com/publications/SteinSwanMBTITheory_2019.pdf

6. Clayton M. Christensen, *The Innovator's Dilemma: When New Technologies Cause Great Firms to Fail* (Boston, MA: Harvard Business School Press, 1997), p. X.

   David Epstein, *Range* (London: Macmillan, 2019)

7. Reference to follow

8. Reference to follow

9. https://www.forbes.com/sites/sunniegiles/2018/05/09/how-vuca-is-reshaping-the-business-environment-and-what-it-means-for-innovation/

10. https://www.forbes.com/sites/johnkotter/2011/07/19/can-you-handle-an-exponential-rate-of-change/?sh=b89470d4eb05

11. https://www.icaew.com/insights/features/archive/fifth-of-ftse-100-ceos-are-accountants

12. Malcolm Gladwell, *Outliers: The Story of Success* (London: Penguin, 2008).

13. Reference to follow - Where is this from? If it's from *Outliers* again, please add ', as Gladwell outlines,' after 'constant'. If it's from elsewhere, please add a new ref.

14. Stuart E. Dreyfus and Hubert L. Dreyfus, "A Five-Stage Model of the Mental Activities Involved in Direct Skill Acquisition," University of California, Berkeley, Operations Research Center (February 1980), https://apps.dtic.mil/sti/pdfs/ADA084551.pdf.

15. Kevin Kruse, "The 80/20 Rule and How It Can Change Your Life" (*Forbes*), last modified 7 March 2016, https://www.forbes.com/sites/kevinkruse/2016/03/07/80-20-rule.

16. Stuart E. Dreyfus and Hubert L. Dreyfus, "A Five-Stage Model of the Mental Activities Involved in Direct Skill Acquisition," University of California, Berkeley, Operations Research Center (February 1980), https://apps.dtic.mil/sti/pdfs/ADA084551.pdf.

17. See, for example, Marcel Schwantes, "This Well-Known Steve Jobs Trait Is What Separates Successful People From Everyone Else" (Inc.), last modified 22 November 2022, https://www.inc.com/marcel-schwantes/this-well-known-steve-jobs-trait-is-what-separates-successful-people-from-everyone-else.html.

18. Héctor García and Francesc Miralles, *Ikigai: The Japanese Secret to a Long and Happy Life* (New York: Penguin, 2017).

19. Reference to follow

20. "Narcissistic" (*Merriam-Webster*), accessed 4 July 2023, https://www.merriam-webster.com/dictionary/narcissistic.

21. https://www.sciencedirect.com/topics/neuroscience/cognitive-bias

22. Amy Gallo, *HBR Guide to Dealing with Conflict* (Boston, MA: Harvard Business Review Press, 2017); Robert J. Sutton, *The Asshole Survival Guide: How to Deal with People Who Treat You Like Dirt* (London: Portfolio Penguin, 2017).

23. Quoted in Amy Gallo, "How to Deal with a Mean Colleague" (*Harvard Business Review*), last modified 16 October 2014, https://hbr.org/2014/10/how-to-deal-with-a-mean-colleague.

24. https://www.ilo.org/global/about-the-ilo/newsroom/news/WCMS_841085/lang--en/index.htm

25. Sanyin Siang, "The Future of Work is Relationships" (*Dialogue*), last modified 21 April 2022, https://dialoguereview.com/the-future-of-work-is-relationships.

26. Skye Schooley, "How to Be a Good Manager" (BND), last modified 21 February 2023, https://www.businessnewsdaily.com/6129-good-manager-skills.html.

27. Sudhanshu Palsule, "Leadership in Uncertainty" (Sudhanshu Palsule: Blog), last modified 12 April 2020, https://sudhanshupalsule.com/2020/04/12/leadership-in-uncertainty.

28. Marcus Buckingham, "What Great Managers Do" (*Harvard Business Review*), last modified March 2005, https://hbr.org/2005/03/what-great-managers-do.

29. Quoted in Skye Schooley, "How to Be a Good Manager" (BND), last modified 21 February 2023, https://www.businessnewsdaily.com/6129-good-manager-skills.html.

30. Citing *The Boss Barometer Report UK 2019* (Kimble, 2019), https://www.kimbleapps.com/resources/boss-barometer-survey-uk.

31. Originally proposed by George T. Doran, "There's a S.M.A.R.T. Way to Write Management's Goals and Objectives," *Management Review* 70, no. 11 (1981): 35–36.

32. Quoted in Skye Schooley, "How to Be a Good Manager" (BND), last modified 21 February 2023, https://www.businessnewsdaily.com/6129-good-manager-skills.html.

33. "Coach" (*Cambridge Dictionary*), accessed 4 July 2023, https://dictionary.cambridge.org/dictionary/english/coach.

34. "Coach" (*Merriam-Webster*), accessed 4 July 2023, https://www.merriam-webster.com/dictionary/coach.

35. Quoted in Skye Schooley, "How to Be a Good Manager" (BND), last modified 21 February 2023, https://www.businessnewsdaily.com/6129-good-manager-skills.html.

36. Wayne Norman, "Business Ethics," in *International Encyclopedia of Ethics*, ed. Hugh LaFollette, last modified 1 February 2013, https://onlinelibrary.wiley.com/doi/10.1002/9781444367072.wbiee719.

37. John Rawls, *A Theory of Justice* (Cambridge, MA: Belknap Press, 1971).

38. Na Jeong-ju, "Tongyang Deceived Customers on Bonds" (*The Korea Times*), last modified 10 December 2013, http://www.koreatimes.co.kr/www/biz/2020/06/488_147740.html.

39. Paulo Sotero, "Petrobras Scandal: Brazilian Political Corruption Scandal" (Britannica), last modified 29 September 2022, https://www.britannica.com/event/Petrobras-scandal.

40. Hannah Ellis-Petersen, "1MDB Scandal Explained: A Tale of Malaysia's Missing Billions" (*The Guardian*), last modified 28 July 2020, https://www.theguardian.com/world/2018/oct/25/1mdb-scandal-explained-a-tale-of-malaysias-missing-billions.

41. Tiisetso Motsoeneng and Emma Rumney, "PwC Investigation Finds $7.4 Billion Accounting Fraud at Steinhoff, Company Says" (Reuters), last modified 15 March 2019, https://www.reuters.com/article/us-steinhoff-intln-accounts-idUSKCN1QW2C2.

42. "Explainer: How Nirav Modi Cheated PNB of Rs 14,000 Crore through Fraudulent LoUs" (*The Economic Times*), last modified 9 November 2022, https://economictimes.indiatimes.com/news/india/explainer-how-nirav-modi-cheated-pnb-of-rs-14000-crore-through-fraudulent-lous/articleshow/95410291.cms.

43. Clayton M. Christensen, James Allworth and Karen Dillon, *How Will You Measure Your Life?* (New York: HarperCollins, 2012).

44. To Carl Seeling, 11 March 1952, in *The Ultimate Quotable Einstein*, ed. Alice Calaprice (Princeton, NJ: Princeton University Press, 2011).

ABOUT THE AUTHORS

Yusuf Ameer is an Associate Director in Corporate Finance at Deloitte Australia. His diverse career spans founding, leading and advising businesses in various cities across two continents.

Beginning his career at Maersk, Yusuf later assumed the position of General Manager in a plastic manufacturing venture before stepping into a strategic role at Caltex in South Africa. Fueled by his entrepreneurial drive, he established a consulting firm that specialized in management consulting and Mergers and Acquisitions (M&A) Advisory services.

Yusuf's consulting career continued at Monitor Deloitte, where he worked on strategy and innovation projects in multiple sectors, including mining, financial services, consumer goods and renewable energy. His journey took him to Australia in 2020, where he joined Deloitte's M&A Consulting Services team in Melbourne. Today, he provides M&A Advisory services to mid-market clients within Australia.

Yusuf holds a Bachelor of Commerce with majors in Finance and Economics from the University of Kwa-Zulu Natal, and an MBA from the Henley Business School, University of Reading, UK. In 2017, he completed the prestigious International Leadership Development Programme at the Gordon Institute of Business Science. He is also a CFA® charterholder.

ABOUT THE AUTHORS

Matthew Butler-Adam is Regional Managing Director in the London office of Duke Corporate Education (CE). Passionate about educational innovation and driving sustainable business growth, Matt cultivates relationships and business development for Duke CE. His work at Duke CE has included leading a variety of major client engagements (ranging from $100,000 to $2 million) in Africa and Europe, operating to forge and progress senior relationships with clients implementing major strategic and leadership transformation programmes. He has deep experience of ambitious leadership culture change programmes, having worked with executive committees on strategic advisory initiatives, and has spearheaded Duke CE's accredited programmes portfolio, including significant new digital learning assets and offerings. He currently leads Duke CE's UK client portfolio in Europe, working with senior clients in financial services, pharma and consumer sectors to lead impactful, innovative leadership education and transformation. Inspirational leadership, value creation through both organic and inorganic growth, and digital innovation are a few of his core areas of leadership expertise.

Before joining Duke CE, Matt worked as a management consultant at Bain & Company as well as at Deloitte in the Mergers and Acquisitions advisory team. In these roles, Matt worked across multiple industries, including financial services and private equity, consumer goods, telecommunications, mining and education. Aside from working as a management consultant, Matt was part of the FirstRand Scholarship Group (Financial Services) and supported an education sector deal at Sanari Capital (Private Equity). Matt's work in the South African market was recognized when he was selected as one of the 'Top 200 Young South Africans' by *The Mail & Guardian*.

With a notable research and academic background, Matt graduated with a master's degree in International Education Policy at Harvard University, where he completed research in the education intervention discipline. He earned an additional master's degree in Economics for Development at the University of Oxford, where his research focused on behavioural economics and micro-econometrics; he was awarded the Luca D'Agliano Prize for the best dissertation in his year. Matt earned his foundational degrees from the University of Cape Town in South Africa, where he was awarded a bachelor's degree and a master's degree with honours. Matt is also a triathlete and ice hockey player.